science and religion

opposing viewpoints

science and religion

opposing **viewpoints**

David L. Bender
Bruno Leone

OPPOSING VIEWPOINTS SERIES

*Greenhaven Press

**577 SHOREVIEW PARK ROAD
ST. PAUL, MINNESOTA 55112**

© Copyright 1981 by Greenhaven Press, Inc.

ISBN 0-89908-309-9 Paper Edition
ISBN 0-89908-334-X Library Edition

CONGRESS SHALL MAKE NO LAW... ABRIDGING THE FREEDOM OF SPEECH, OR OF THE PRESS

first amendment to the U.S. Constitution

The basic foundation of our democracy is the first amendment guarantee of freedom of expression. The OPPOSING VIEW-POINTS SERIES is dedicated to the concept of this basic freedom and the idea that it is more important to practice it than to enshrine it.

TABLE OF CONTENTS Page

the Opposing viewpoints series

THE IMPORTANCE OF EXAMINING OPPOSING VIEWPOINTS

The purpose of this book, and the Opposing Viewpoints Series as a whole, is to confront you with alternative points of view on complex and sensitive issues.

Perhaps the best way to inform yourself is to analyze the positions of those who are regarded as experts and well studied on the issues. It is important to consider every variety of opinion in an attempt to determine the truth. Opinions from the mainstream of society should be examined. Also important are opinions that are considered radical, reactionary, minority or stigmatized by some other uncomplimentary label. An important lesson of history is the fact that many unpopular and even despised opinions eventually gained widespread acceptance. The opinions of Socrates, Jesus and Galileo are good examples of this.

You will approach this book with opinions of your own on the issues debated within it. To have a good grasp of your own viewpoint you must understand the arguments of those with whom you disagree. It is said that those who do not completely understand their adversary's point of view do not fully understand their own.

Perhaps the most persuasive case for considering opposing viewpoints has been presented by John Stuart Mill in his work *On Liberty*. Consider the following statements of his when studying controversial issues.

THE OPINIONS OF OTHERS

If all mankind minus one were of one opinion, and only one person were of the contrary opinion, mankind would be no more justified in silencing that one person than he, if he had the power, would be justified in silencing mankind....

We can never be sure that the opinion we are endeavoring to stifle is a false opinion...

All silencing of discussion is an assumption of infallibility....

Ages are no more infallible than individuals; every age having held many opinions which subsequent ages have deemed not only false but absurd; and it is as certain that many opinions now general will be rejected by future ages....

The only way in which a human being can make some approach to knowing the whole of a subject, is by hearing what can be said about it by persons of every variety of opinion, and studying all modes in which it can be looked at by every character of mind. No wise man ever acquired his wisdom in any mode but this....

The beliefs which we have most warrant for have no safeguard to rest on but a standing invitation to the whole world to prove them unfounded....

To call any proposition certain, while there is any one who would deny its certainty if permitted, but who is not permitted, is to assume that we ourselves and those who agree with us are the judges of certainty, and judges without hearing the other side....

Men are not more zealous for truth than they are for error, and a sufficient application of legal or even social penalties will generally succeed in stopping the propagation of either....

However unwilling a person who has a strong opinion may admit the possibility that his opinion may be false, he ought to be moved by the consideration that, however true it may be, if it is not fully, frequently, and fearlessly discussed, it will be a dead dogma, not a living truth.

From *On Liberty* by John Stuart Mill

A pitfall to avoid in considering alternative points of view is that of regarding your own point of view as being merely common sense and the most rational stance, and the point of view of others as being only opinion and naturally wrong. It may be that the opinion of others is correct and that yours is in error.

Another pitfall to avoid is that of closing your mind to the opinions of those whose views differ from yours. The best way to approach a dialogue is to make your primary purpose that of understanding the mind and arguments of the other person and not that of enlightening him or her with your solutions. One learns more by listening than by speaking.

It is my hope that after reading this book you will have a deeper understanding of the issues debated and will appreciate the complexity of even seemingly simple issues when good and honest people disagree. This awareness is particularly important in a democratic society such as ours, where people enter into public debate to determine the common good. People with whom you disagree should not be regarded as enemies, but rather as friends who suggest a different path to a common goal.

ANALYZING SOURCES OF INFORMATION

The Opposing Viewpoints Series uses diverse sources; magazines, journals, books, newspapers, statements and position papers from a wide range of individuals and organizations. These sources help in the development of a mindset that is open to the consideration of a variety of opinions.

The format of the Opposing Viewpoints Series should help you answer the following questions.

1. *Are you aware that three of the most popular weekly news magazines, Time, Newsweek, and U.S. News and World Report are not totally objective accounts of the news?*
2. **Do you know there is no such thing as a completely objective author, book, newspaper or magazine?**
3. **Do you think that because a magazine or newspaper article is unsigned it is always a statement of facts rather than opinions?**
4. **How can you determine the point of view of newspapers and magazines?**
5. **When you read do you question an author's frame of reference (political persuasion, training, and life experience)?**

Many people finish their formal education unable to cope with these basic questions. They have little chance to understand the social forces and issues surrounding them. Some fall easy victims to demagogues preaching solutions to problems by scapegoating minorities with conspiratorial and paranoid explanations of complex social issues.

I do not want to imply that anything is wrong with authors and publications that have a political slant or bias. All authors have a frame of reference. Readers should understand this. You should also understand that almost all writers have a point of view. An important skill in reading is to be able to locate and identify a point of view. This series gives you practice in both.

DEVELOPING BASIC THINKING SKILLS

A number of basic skills for critical thinking are practiced in the discussion activities that appear throughout the books in the series. Some of the skills are:

Locating a Point of View The ability to determine which side of an issue an author supports.

Evaluating Sources of Information The ability to choose from among alternative sources the most reliable and accurate source in relation to a given subject.

Distinguishing Between Primary and Secondary Sources The ability to understand the important distinction between sources which are primary (original or eyewitness accounts) and those which are secondary (historically removed from, and based on, primary sources).

Separating Fact from Opinion The ability to make the basic distinction between factual statements (those which can be demonstrated or verified empirically) and statements of opinion (those which are beliefs or attitudes that cannot be proved).

Distinguishing Between Prejudice and Reason The ability to differentiate between statements of prejudice (unfavorable, preconceived judgments based on feelings instead of reason) and statements of reason (conclusions that can be clearly and logically explained or justified).

Identifying Stereotypes The ability to identify oversimplified, exaggerated descriptions (favorable or unfavorable) about people and insulting statements about racial, religious or national groups, based upon misinformation or lack of information.

Recognizing Ethnocentrism The ability to recognize attitudes or opinions that express the view that one's own race, culture, or group is inherently superior, or those attitudes that judge another race, culture, or group in terms of one's own.

It is important to consider opposing viewpoints. It is equally important to be able to critically analyze those viewpoints. The discussion activities in this book will give you practice in mastering these thinking skills.

Using this book, and others in the series, will help you develop critical thinking skills. These skills should improve your ability to better understand what you read. You should be better able to separate fact from opinion, reason from rhetoric. You should become a better consumer of information in our media-centered culture.

A VALUES ORIENTATION

Throughout the Opposing Viewpoints Series you are presented conflicting values. A good example is *American Foreign Policy*. The first chapter debates whether foreign policy should be based on the same kind of moral principles that individuals use in guiding their personal actions, or instead be based primarily on doing what best advances national interests, regardless of moral implications.

The series does not advocate a particular set of values. Quite the contrary! The very nature of the series leaves it to you, the reader, to formulate the values orientation that you find most suitable. My purpose, as editor of the series, is to see that this is made possible by offering a wide range of viewpoints which are fairly presented.

David L. Bender
Opposing Viewpoints Series Editor

SCIENCE AND RELIGION

"The Bible was written to show us how to go to heaven, not how the heavens go."

Galileo Galilei (1564–1642)

In the spring of 1633, Galileo Galilei, an Italian scientist, was delivered before the dreaded Roman Inquisition to be tried on charges of heresy. He was denounced, according to a formal statement, "for holding as true the false doctrine ... that the sun is the center of the world and immovable, and that the earth moves." The statement went on to read that "the proposition that the sun is the center of the world and does not move from its place is absurd and...heretical, because it is expressly contrary to the Holy Scripture." Galileo was found guilty and forced to renounce his views. Ill and broken in spirit, he was sentenced to a life of perpetual imprisonment and penance.

Throughout history, Galileo has been joined by others in what is viewed by many as an ongoing conflict between science and religion. Roger Bacon, a 13th century English priest, spent the final 14 years of his life in a dungeon for writing that in the quest for truth, experimentation and observation are valid challenges to the uncritical acceptance of spiritual and secular authorities. In the 19th century, Charles Darwin was mocked and maligned for claiming that all living things evolved from lower life forms. And in 1925, John Scopes, a high school biology teacher from Dayton, Tennessee, was accused and convicted of violating a state law which specified that only divine creation, as an explanation for the origin of life, could be taught in Tennessee public schools.

In an age in which science and technology have become such dominant forces in human progress, these examples seem like barbaric remnants of an unenlightened past. The truth, however, is that the conflict between science and religion is still being waged. The "battlefield" has changed, the "weapons" have been updated and the "wounds" inflicted are generally less gaping. But the battle goes on!

All of this would seem to raise two very relevant questions. First, why are science and religion at odds? And second, have they always been and will they continue to be antagonists?

The answer to the first question is apparent. Both science and religion seek to provide answers to some very fundamental questions related to the physical world. How did life originate? In what direction, if any, is life heading? Can we define human nature and satisfactorily explain human behavior? The fact that scientists and theologians usually arrive at different answers to these and similar questions is not the problem. Scientists often heatedly disagree even among themselves over basic questions of cause and effect. The same is true of theologians. Rather, the difficulty lies in the vastly contrasting approaches employed by each in finding answers to these seminal questions. Science climbs the ladder of reason in its search for truth while religion kneels before the altar of faith. The methodology of science includes observation and experimentation while religion embraces divine revelation. Thus as the physical anthropologist attempts to explain human origins in terms of progressive evolution, the minister may look no further than the creative act in Genesis I. Similarly, as the psychologist explains warfare as a species "death wish," the theologian explains it as the price paid for "original sin."

The reader should not conclude from the above that science and religion cannot be reconciled. Indeed, and to answer our second question, for centuries religion has had many staunch defenders in the scientific community and vice versa. This is especially true in more recent times. For example, scientists such as the late Wernher von Braun (see Chapter 1, Viewpoint 4), one of the early leaders of America's space program, claim that modern science and technology, by unfolding the mysteries of nature, verify the handiwork of a Divine Creator. More specifically, academics like Harold G. Coffin (see Chapter 3, Viewpoint 4), a professor of paleontology at Andrews University in Michigan, have been utilizing the tools of modern science to help prove biblical claims of a six-day creation and a comparatively young earth. Moreover, many contemporary biblical scholars, by rejecting the literal interpretation of such biblical passages as the six-day creation, have managed to reconcile God and at least one highly controversial scientific theory. Evolution, they suggest, simply may be part of the Divine Plan (see Chapter 3, Viewpoint 7).

This anthology of OPPOSING VIEWPOINTS attempts to deal with several relevant questions in the Science/Religion controversy. The editors have compiled readings from a broad range of knowledgeable sources including scientists, editorialists, teachers, laypersons and clergy. However, one final and significant point is worth noting. While the viewpoints are largely related to the Judeo-Christian or Western religious tradition, the concepts and issues upon which they focus would seem to apply to virtually all corners of the world. Although science and religion may be shrouded by differing cultural traditions, the cornerstone of each, reason and faith, can never be disguised nor denied.

Chapter

science
and
religion

Are Science
and Religion
Compatible?

Friends or Foes?

"The supernatural has no support in science, it is incompatible with science, it is frequently an active foe of science."

Science and Religion Are Not Compatible

Anton J. Carlson

Anton J. Carlson (1875–1956), a native of Sweden, was a renowned and widely respected scientist. He immigrated to the United States in 1891 where he eventually earned his Ph.D. from Stanford University. A former president of the American Association for the Advancement of Science, Dr. Carlson's extensive research on diabetes contributed to the development and manufacture of insulin. In 1953, the American Medical Association voted him humanitarian of the year and awarded him its distinguished service gold medal. In the following viewpoint, Dr. Carlson equates religion with primitive superstition and concludes that religion is "frequently an active foe of science."

Consider the following questions while reading:
1. According to Carlson, what is the scientific method?
2. List some of the examples Carlson offers of supernatural events which are contrary to known processes in nature.
3. Why is Carlson critical of "supernatural ethics?"
4. Do you agree with Carlson that science and religion are not compatible? Why or why not?

"Science and the Supernatural", Carlson, A.J., *Scientific Monthly*, Vol. 73, pp. 217–225, 27 February 1931.

SCIENCE

The most important element in science appears to be the scientific method. What is the method of science? In essence it is this—the rejection *in toto* of all non-observational and non-experimental authority in the field of experience. No matter how high in state, church, society or science the individual may be who makes pronouncement on any subject, the scientists always ask for the evidence. When no evidence is produced, other than "revelations" in dreams, or the "voice of God," the scientists can pay no attention whatsoever, except to ask: How do they get that way? If evidence is produced, he proceeds to examine the evidence. Does the evidence justify the conclusions of statements made? There is nothing abstruse in the method of science . . .

The principle of the scientific method, in fact, is only a refinement, by analysis and controls, of the universal process of learning by experience . . .

TRIAL AND ERROR

It seems that the supernatural in the sense of religions or a religious attitude toward nature and life is nearly universal among men at some stage of development. Science in the sense of elements of the scientific method, the learning by experience, is even more universal. It antedates man. The amoeba appears to work in part by the principle of trial and error; so do some of the higher animals, including the ape. This type of reaction or behavior in the simpler forms of animal life does not necessarily connote conscious associative memories, but there is no good reason for denying the latter factor in the higher animals. The trial and error method is direct experience . . .

THE SUPERNATURAL AS A WAY TO KNOWLEDGE

By supernatural we understand information, theories, beliefs and practices claiming origins other than verifiable experiences and thinking, or events contrary to known processes in nature, such as the production of wine from water alone; the resurrection from the dead of persons in advanced stages of decomposition; accounts of creation of the world and of man by people who were not present at these events, and not in a position to infer from cosmic data; specific codes of behavior enunciated to some man by some anthropomorphic god; arrest of the course of the sun through space so that the Jewish army could see to kill a few more natives; casting devils out of men, and sending demons into hogs; human pregnancies solely through non-material, that is, divine agencies; perpetual recurrence of a species of "immaculate conception" in that a divinity sends embryonic "souls" into every human fetus either at the moment of union of sperm and ova, or later in intra-uterine life, etc., *ad infinitum, ad absurdum, ad nauseum.* This supernatural has been presented to man with varying degrees of clarity in a great variety of books and sermons by prophets, priests, and other holy men, in addition to the information in so-called sacred books, such as the Bible, the Koran, the Vedas and the Book of Mormon . . .

PARADOX OF RELIGION AND SCIENCE

The best therapy for gullibility and unbridled imagination is the development of the critical use of the scientific attitude... The paradox is that so many people are willing to abandon their practical intelligence when they enter fields of religion or ethics.

Paul Kurtz, *The Humanist,* July/August, 1976

REVELATIONS CLOUD KNOWLEDGE

What has science to say to all this? The most serious aspect of the supernatural is, not the revelations, *per se,* the miracles, the myths and the guesses, but the injunction that all this **must be taken on faith**, that inquiry and doubt is tabu — that is, sin. A good deal of "revealed" information about the nature of the world and the nature of man has proved entirely erroneous. So far as the nature of the world and of man is concerned the revelations appear to be nothing but what could have been projected as guesses by any human contemporary of the revelations, on the basis of the knowledge and the ignorance of those times. The "revelations" have been of no aid in the advance of real knowledge of cosmogony, physiology, physics, chemistry or disease. **On the contrary**, they have, through human stupidity and obscenity frequently aided in retardation. The revelations to Joseph

Smith (the Book of Mormon), the repeated revelations by Jehovah to Brigham Young, and the rise of Christian Science are recent. The character, education, intelligence and environment of the people concerned are fairly well known. In the light of all the known facts in these instances, is there any intelligent man or woman today, not steeped in childhood in the lore of Mormonism or Christian Science, who can have any respect for such revelations as a source of knowledge? When the Mormon leaders received a tip from God that polygamy was ordered by him for his chosen people on earth (by the way, a revelation that is easy to take by the average human male), the United States Government did not hesitate to challenge God, or Brigham Young's sanity and veracity. The Federal Government was powerful and adamant and God yielded through a second revelation to the effect that he had changed his mind and polygamy was no longer according to the plan of God! In some cases the "revelations" are reported as coming through dreams; in other cases through brush fires; by direct writing of the finger of God on stones, or indirectly through oracles, popes, the flight of birds and the liver of slaughtered bulls . . .

Most of the weird stories of creation of the universe, animals, man, of divine or demoniacal control of natural forces, of disease, etc., that have come to us via the supernatural route run contrary to facts now known, or rendered untenable, as possibilities, by known facts . . .

FAITH AND LOGIC

God-believers and believers in witches are closer than many of us realize. Not only do they both appeal to faith, but by virtue of this appeal, they have in effect rejected the use of logic and experience.

Marvin Zimmerman, *The Humanist,* July/August, 1976

THE ETHICS OF THE SUPERNATURAL

May I make a few concluding remarks on the ethics of the supernatural, speaking not as a scientist but as a common man? The ethics of science is simple: absolute honesty in recording and presenting data, and curbing wishes, personal prejudices and emotions by reason in interpreting data.

There appears to be a great variety of ethics in the supernatural. Looking upon the supernatural simply as man's stumbling attempts at learning, at adjustments, as flounderings toward greater happiness, as quests for explanations of the unknown, this variety is both inevitable and understandable. From this point of view, the modern man of science has no essential quarrels with Jesus, Confucius, Zoroaster, or Buddha. They did the best they could, considering the ignorance of their times. We can do no more. But now and then individual champions of the supernatural have been either unusually stupid or inordinately selfish and cruel. The judgement of posterity will be severe on the men who coerced Galileo and their brethren of today who know or might know, yet rivet the shackles of supernaturalism on the human mind. For they sin against man. It is significant that neither Jesus nor his apostles appear to have claimed any supernatural authority or absolute wisdom for their sayings or writings. The ignoble doctrine of divine revelation of absolute truth for all times appears to be a later invention. But in Mormonism and Mohammedanism it is present with the founders. I said: ignoble doctrine. Intellectual tyranny is to me as immoral as physical tyranny. Stifling freedom of inquiry and of thinking by religious tabus or legal dicta appears to me highly immoral . . . Science nurtures inquiry, the supernatural stifles it . . .

THE SUPERNATURAL IS INCOMPATIBLE WITH SCIENCE

As I see it, the supernatural has no support in science, it is incompatible with science, it is frequently an active foe of science. It is unnecessary for the good life. And yet, the supernatural, in varying dilutions, is likely to persist in society for a very long time. The unconditioning and reconditioning of mankind in fundamentals has been a slow process in the past. It may go a little faster in the future. It is a matter of forgetting the hypothetical universe created out of ignorance and motivated by our disciplined emotions; and a reconditioning to the actual universe, as gradually understood through controlled experience and experiment.

"True science is the handmaiden of true theology."

Science and Religion Are Compatible

Ronald H. Russell

The *Journal of the American Scientific Affiliation* is a publication whose editorial policy attempts to underline the harmony which exists between science and religion. Many of the Journal's articles are written by Christian scientists affiliated with major universities throughout the world. The following viewpoint, by Ronald H. Russell, was originally entitled "A Christian Looks At Science" when it appeared in the Journal. The author is of the opinion that science and religion, though operating in different spheres, "truly . . . complement one another."

Consider the following questions while reading:

1. **What are John Dewey's five phases of the "scientific road?"**
2. **What is the author's attitude toward theologians who attempt to "scientifically prove God?"**
3. **Do you agree with Russell's conclusion that "careful science and true theology complement one another?" Why or why not?**

Ronald H. Russell, "A Christian Looks at Science", *Journal of the American Scientific Affiliation,* December, 1958. Reprinted with permission of the American Scientific Affiliation, P.O. Box 862, Elgin, IL 60120.

There are many major matters about which people are not in total agreement. Sometimes these divergencies are mild and innocuous while in other instances these schisms are deep and fundamental. This diversity of opinion clearly manifests itself when individuals with shallow talk supported with equally shallow thinking affirm that a definite conflict exists between science and theology. Unfortunately we do have pseudo–scientists and pseudo–theologians; however, it is my belief that true science is the handmaiden of true theology.

Let us consider for a moment the method of science, that is, the scientific method . . .

DEWEY'S SCIENTIFIC ROAD

The scientific road has five phases which John Dewey calls (1) Suggestion, (2) Intellectualization, (3) The Guiding Idea or Hypothesis, (4) Reasoning in a Narrower Sense and (5) Testing and Verifying or Disproving the Hypothesis by Experimentation. Scientific knowledge is grounded in sensation. If a scientist had no sense receptors he would be forced out of the field of research . . .

The scientist should not deviate from that which he cannot see, hear, smell, taste, or feel. He says, "I know" because he can say, "I have seen." My conviction on the existence of Euglena in a drop of water depended on faith until January 1956. Before that date I had read about them in books. I had been told by people that such organisms existed. But during that month I looked through a microscope and saw a Euglena. Of course, I still have to accept on faith the testimony of my instructor that what I witnessed darting about in the field of vision was a Euglena. But I am no longer on *a priori* grounds. I recognized it as having life because I saw it move.

ROLE OF SCIENCE

Since sensory experience is prerequisite to conviction, science has nothing to say on questions, the proving or disproving of which does not involve experimentation. Science can neither affirm nor deny the existence of God and the unseen world about us. Science cannot affirm that a miracle is impossible because if there is a God then a miracle is possible and science cannot dogmatically deny the existence of God...

How can science constantly deny the existence of God? They don't know, and therefore cannot say. But they can say,

"As far as we know, there is no God—but we don't know very far. There may be a God, but He is unknown to science." Because science can never ultimately arrive she should humbly remain within the restricted limits she has set for herself.

ROLE OF RELIGION

On the other hand, the theologian who stoops to an attempt to "scientifically prove God" is, to say the least, doing that which is grossly unnecessary. Why turn your back on the higher knowledge of faith and submit the case to a lower and less trustworthy court? Shall I prove God by science? Not I. I affirm God, Christ, Creation, Sin, Salvation, Miracles, Heaven and Hell on the grounds of God–given and sustaining faith. And after my affirmation, if any scientist forgets his restricted limitations and attempts to challenge me, I shall take his own scientific method and use it to drive him back to his own back yard which is so effectively enclosed by the fences of sense perception. The best argument against the objective existence of the unseen is only negative argument. Let science therefore concern herself with an exploitation of the visible world and leave the metaphysical and theological field to her betters . . .

RELIGIOUS AND SCIENTIFIC THOUGHT

The history of science itself reveals the fact that the religious and the scientific sides of human thought are not inconsistent with each other, but are complementary in the whole man.

Mendel Sachs, *The Humanist,* November/December, 1976

COMPLEMENTARY ROLES

Science in her place is capable of tremendous good. The narrow–minded preacher who runs for office on a platform of "All Scientists in Hell" had better think twice and remain silent, or else drive the horse and carriage instead of his new Chrysler or Ford, because it was science, not religion that built his automobile. Theology is good in its place, but theology under the hood of a car is out of place. There the preacher needs thermodynamics. If it is better to push a button than light a wick, dial a radio than crank a phonograph, go United than oxcart—then science should stand up and take a bow.

SCIENTIST AND BELIEVER

There is something in the Christian gospel that is similar to what we find in nature, and as a scientist I find this reassuring. The gospel may be puzzling and not completely understandable, but it shows signs of having the same Maker as nature.

John A. McIntyre, *The Appeal of Christianity to a Scientist*

There is much knowledge available on the level of the mature mind, unaided by revelation. We as Christians ought to seek that knowledge. We should utilize our God–given faculties which are available, namely sensory perception and natural reason. This is Science. When followed carefully, it yields tremendous dividends. Truly careful science and true theology complement one another.

"Religion is not science's sibling, Atheism is . . . Atheism grows stronger with each new advance of science."

Science Verifies Atheism

G. Richard Bozarth

The *American Atheist* magazine is published monthly by the Society of Separationists, Austin, Texas. (Its Editor-in-Chief, Madalyn Murray O'Hair, is often referred to as the "best known atheist in the world today.") The magazine frequently features articles which emphasize the alleged scientific contradictions inherent in religion. The following viewpoint, by G. Richard Bozarth, is typical of its science/religion pieces. The growth of science, the author contends, is slowly "reducing the mystery" which feeds religion.

Consider the following questions while reading:
1. **According to the author, what happens to religion each time "science clears up a mystery?" Do you agree? Why or why not?**
2. **Why does Bozarth believe that atheism, and not religion, is the "sister" of science?**

G. Richard Bozarth, "Whose Sister Is Science?", *The American Atheist,* May, 1978. Reprinted with permission of the publisher.

A Christian I used to correspond with had one particular opinion that he often expressed. This opinion was that religion and science are sisters. He endeavored to convince me of this by making examples of scientists who were also religionists. For instance, he quoted Wernher von Braun as having said, "I just can't envision this whole universe coming into being without something like a divine will."

Are religion and science sisters? This is a necessary question for an Atheist to answer, and at first glance, the answer seems to be yes. After all, in the ranks of religion there have been and now are many, many scientists, some of them the great geniuses who have revolutionized human concepts of the nature of the universe. Surely, if scientists can also be religionists, then religion and science must be sisters . . .

SCIENCE AND RELIGION

Some people enjoy discovering the secrets of nature, and these people become scientists if they can. A scientist like von Braun, who would design rockets for any nation that would finance his work, is certainly not going to give up his profession for the religion he needs. What does he or she do?

The scientist who is also a religionist does not say, "Science has been and is religion's worst enemy, so I cannot be a scientist and help science in its victory over religion." Such a scientist normally won't surrender his or her enjoyable profession. He or she will reconcile religion and science in his or her own mind, and call them sisters. This is necessary for the religious scientist . . .

MORTAL ENEMIES

We must not allow ourselves to be deceived by the pious words of religious scientists into believing science and religion are sisters. To grasp what science means to religion, we must go beyond the individual reconciliations of religionists who are also scientists. To a great many religionists who are not scientists, science is the tool and breeding ground of Atheism. The most persistent stereotype characteristic of the scientist, after sloppy absentmindedness, is Atheism. Father Shipman, one of the local priests in Vacaville, Calif., once declared that Atheism is "chiefly found" in moral degenerates and "among students of physical science." (*The Reporter*, 17 April 77) Now, is that any way to talk about your sister?

Why, considering the numbers of scientists who were and

Cover of *American Atheist* magazine, July, 1980. Reprinted with permission.

are devout religionists, has this stereotype of the scientist being Atheist become so widely accepted?

Religion requires mystery. "The Christian rather rejoices in mystery, reveling in the triumphant paradoxes of revelation," George Brand writes in *Catholicism* (p. 80). A mystery, according to Webster's Third New International Dictionary, is "something that has not been or cannot be explained."

In other words, where there is mystery there is ignorance; where there is mystery, there you can find god offered as an explanation to fill the void of ignorance. Prehistorical humans invented gods to answer the mysteries of nature, and invented religions as a means to influence divine will.

What is mystery's mortal enemy? Science! Every time science clears up a mystery, explains the heretofore unexplainable, a little of religion's realm is taken from it. Each time science pushes the boundaries of our ignorance back a little, god has less territory in the human mind to roam in.

FAITH VS REASON

Science is based on reason. Religion is based on faith. The increase of the influence of one means a decrease in the influence of the other.

Madalyn Murray O'Hair, *American Atheist,* March, 1981

SCIENCE AND ATHEISM

Religion resents this because science slowly, steadily is reducing the mystery that nurtures religion. Consequently, despite individual reconciliation, religion's greatest foe is science . . .

Religion is not science's sibling, Atheism is! Atheism is the only philosophy that has nothing to fear from science because Atheism grows stronger with each new advance of science.

Perhaps it is better to describe Atheism as the child of science, because nowhere in all history will one find Atheism so diffused throughout a society that a movement and organization like the American Atheists was possible, except in 20th century America—except in the most scientific country of this most scientific century of human existence. Atheism abhors ignorance. So does science. It is natural that they should flourish together . . .

As our civilization becomes increasingly scientific, where will we find a moral and ethical system that is compatible with science and helps us to progress as human beings capable of dealing with science's progress? Will that system continue to be the one offered by religion? No. Religion's constant battle against science is the major reason so many people feel distrustful of science and are unable to adapt to this age of science we live in. Religion can only survive by degenerating our confidence in science, and religion has succeeded in this with far too many.

"You cannot build a wall between science and religion."

Science Verifies God

Wernher von Braun

Dr. Wernher von Braun (1912–1977) was one of the leading forces behind America's space program. Director of the George C. Marshall Space Flight Center for many years, the German-born scientist was considered one of the world's leading rocket and space authorities. Dr. von Braun's published works include: *Across the Space Frontier* and *First Men to the Moon*. In the following viewpoint, he expresses an opinion he held throughout most of his adult life, namely, that scientific advancement serves to unfold the mysteries of God's creation.

Consider the following questions while reading:
1. **What does the author mean when he writes that "science and religion are sisters?"**
2. **What is the author's attitude with regard to the following statement?: "Let science investigate the physical world, while religion explains spiritual matters."**
3. **Why does the author consider science a "religious activity?"**

Wernher von Braun, "Science as Religious Activity". Published in *All Believers Are Brothers*, ed. Roland Gammon. Reprinted with permission of Maria von Braun.

The two most powerful forces shaping our civilization today are science and religion. Through science man strives to learn more of the mysteries of creation. Through religion he seeks to know the Creator.

SCIENCE AND RELIGION ARE SISTERS

Neither operates independently. It is as difficult for me to understand a scientist who does not acknowledge the presence of a superior rationality behind the existence of the universe as it is to comprehend a theologian who would deny the advances of science. Far from being independent or opposing forces, science and religion are sisters. Both seek a better world. While science seeks control over the forces of nature around us, religion controls the forces of nature within us . . .

SCIENCE DOES NOT POSSESS ULTIMATE TRUTH

Today thousands of scientists all over the world are engaged in the greatest intellectual adventure ever undertaken by man: attempting to understand the origin and functioning of a physical universe that is vast in space and time, complicated in detail, and awesome in its orderliness. Thus, to say that science's only purpose is trying to discover physical laws to increase man's control over the forces of nature is no longer an adequate explanation of science's goal; for, the concept of science itself has grown. The raw material of science is a set of experiences, observations, and measurements with which the scientist attempts to build a model of time, space, and matter. When new knowledge is discovered, the old model is not discarded; it is simply changed according to the pattern of relationships which the scientist finds in this set of experiences.

By his willingness to change his model, or his concepts, the scientist is simply admitting that he makes no claim to possessing ultimate truth. His scientific laws are essentially descriptions of his observations. Scientific laws do not control reality, but merely try to explain it; therefore, the laws may be changed when new knowledge is revealed . . .

The scientist works in an atmosphere where doubt is an accepted way of life, and unnecessary authority rejected. Thomas Huxley has said of the scientist: "For him scepticism is the highest of duties; blind faith the unpardonable sin." The rise of science has been accompanied by a loss of tradition, which has been the mainstay of faith. Clashes between science and religion have therefore been frequent. And yet, it

"And the firmament showeth His handiwork."

The *Pleiades* Star Cluster. Courtesy of the Yerkes Observatory, the University of Chicago.

is one of the greatest tragedies of our times that science and religion have been cast as antagonists. To resolve the conflict, it has been tempting to adopt a policy of peaceful co-existence, and divide our experience into two parts, granting science control over one part, and permitting religion its authority in the other.

GOD THROUGH SCIENCE

True science discovers God in an ever-increasing degree as though God were waiting behind every door opened by science.

Pope Pius XII, Pontifical Academy of Science, 1951

SCIENCE AND RELIGION EXPLAIN THE SAME REALITY

Let science investigate the physical world, while religion explains spiritual matters, this argument goes. When science gets to the end of its rope, let faith take over to account for the unexplainable. This is a fatal step. Two separate worlds for science and religion might work if no scientist were ever a Christian, and no Christian were ever a scientist. But science and religion do not operate in separate realms.

You cannot build a wall between science and religion. As science explains more of the intriguing mysteries of life and the universe, its realms expand into those areas which previously were either unknown or accepted solely by faith. Every experience we have—physical or spiritual—must fit together into a pattern that is credible and meaningful. Man is the observer of the universe, the experimenter, the searcher for truth, but he is not spectator alone. He is a participant in the continuing process of creation. He is the highest product of that creation. And he is directly affected as more and more of the wonders of that creation are unveiled.

Science and religion may be compared to two windows in a house, through which we may observe the world about us—or our neighbors. (And there are other windows, such as art, literature and history.) Whatever we observe through any of the windows in this allegorical house must fit into our model of the universe and our place in it. If it does not fit, we must revise our model, change our thinking, broaden our understanding of creation.

SCIENCE: A RELIGIOUS ACTIVITY

In our modern world many people seem to feel that our rapid advances in the field of science render such things as religious beliefs untimely or old-fashioned. They wonder why we should be satisfied in "believing" something, when science tells us that we "know" so many things. The simple answer to this contention is that we know many more mysteries of nature today than when the age of scientific enlightenment began. There is certainly no scientific reason why God cannot retain the same position in our modern world that he held before we began probing His creation with telescope and cyclotron.

SCIENCE REVEALS GOD

When science is true to its mission, and becomes the handmaiden of religion, opening doors through which the splendor and grace of God may come to man, unbelievable and undreamed-of glories may yet flood the world of tomorrow.

Joseph R. Sizoo, from *All Believers Are Brothers,* ed., Roland Gammon

---

While science is not a religion, it is a religious activity by its presuppositions, its method of working, and its search for truth. The Creator is revealed through His creation. As Charles A. Coulson says, "Science is helping to put a face on God." We should remember that science exists only because there are people, and its concepts exist only in the minds of men. Behind these concepts lies Reality—revealed to us only by the grace of God.

DISTINGUISHING BETWEEN STATEMENTS THAT ARE PROVABLE AND THOSE THAT ARE NOT

From various sources of information we are constantly confronted with statements and generalizations about social and moral problems. In order to think clearly about these problems, it is useful if one can make a basic distinction between statements for which evidence can be found, and other statements which cannot be verified because evidence is not available, or the issue is so controversial that it cannot be definitely proved. Students should constantly be aware that social studies texts and other sources often contain statements of a controversial nature. The following exercise is designed to allow you to experiment with statements that are provable and those that are not.

In each of the following statements indicate whether you believe it is provable (P), too controversial to be proved to everyone's satisfaction (C), or unprovable because of the lack of evidence (U). Compare and discuss your results with your classmates.

P = Provable
C = Too Controversial
U = Unprovable

_____ 1. Science can neither affirm nor deny the existence of God.

_____ 2. Science and religion are sisters. Both seek a better world.

_____ 3. God-believers and believers in witches are closer than many of us realize.

_____ 4. If scientists have learned anything from the theologians, it is that they too must approach the mysteries of nature with awe – and humility.

_____ 5. Most western religions accept the evolution theory as the creative process throughout natural history.

_____ 6. Science is designed to tell us the what and how of natural phenomena; the Bible tells us who and why.

_____ 7. There is no question that genetic engineering has spiritual ramifications.

_____ 8. Advances in science have increased life expectancy and generally made life easier for a majority of humankind.

_____ 9. There is no such thing as "responsible" engineering of new forms and combinations of life.

_____ 10. To cut off research because of fear of the possibilities inherent in knowledge is to condemn our society to a life without creativity.

_____ 11. Science has proven that the Universe exploded into being at a certain moment.

_____ 12. True science discovers God in an ever-increasing degree as though God were waiting behind every door opened by science.

BIBLIOGRAPHY

The editors have compiled the following list of periodical articles which deal with the subject matter of this chapter. The majority of periodicals listed are available in most school and public libraries.

Rochelle Albin and Donald D. Montagna — *Mystical Aspects of Science,* **The Humanist,** March/April, 1977, p. 44.

John W. Alexander — *The Fall and Rise of a Scientist,* **The Christian Reader,** May/June, 1979, p. 7.

Luther Burbank — *Our Savior, Science,* **The Humanist,** November/December, 1976, p. 53.

Thomas Ferrick — *The World Council of Churches on Science and Faith,* **The Humanist,** November/December, 1979, p. 50.

George S. Hammond — *The Value System in the Scientific Subculture,* **Bulletin of the Atomic Scientists,** December, 1976, p. 36.

T. George Harris — *The Religious War Over Truth and Tools,* **Psychology Today,** January, 1976, p. 67.

H. Harold Hartzler — *How the Study of Science Has Increased My Faith,* **Journal of the American Scientific Affiliation,** December, 1957, p. 7.

Journal of the American Scientific Affiliation — *Towards a Christian View of Science,* March, 1971, p. 1.

Delos B. McKown — *Close Encounters of an Ominous Kind,* **The Humanist,** January/February, 1979, p. 4.

Albert Rosenfeld — *When Man Becomes as God: The Biological Prospect,* **Saturday Review,** December 10, 1977, p. 15.

Mendel Sachs — *On the Complementarity of Science and Religion,* **The Humanist,** November/December, 1976, p. 45.

Carl Sagan — *Science and Religion: 'Similar Objective, Different Methods',* **U.S. News and World Report,** December 1, 1980, p. 62.

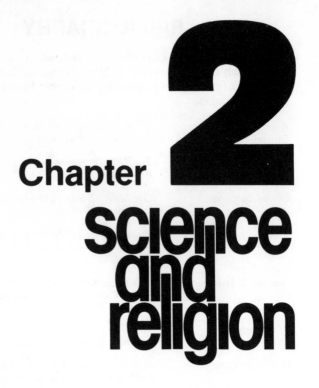

Chapter **2**

science and religion

How Did the Universe Originate?

"In the beginning was the Word."

"In the beginning was the Hydrogen Atom."

The Andromeda Galaxy. Lick Observatory Photograph. Used with permission.

"The scientist has scaled the mountains of ignorance... as he pulls himself over the final rock, he is greeted by a band of theologians who have been sitting there for centuries."

God May Be the Creator

Robert Jastrow

Robert Jastrow is an American scientist of wide fame and impeccable credentials. He received his Ph.D. from Columbia University in theoretical physics. He has researched in the fields of nuclear physics, planetary science and atmospheric physics and received the NASA Medal for Exceptional Scientific Achievement. Yet Dr. Jastrow invited the scorn of many fellow scientists with the publication of his book, *God and the Astronomers*. In that work, Jastrow suggests that God may be the possible cause of the "Big Bang" which brought the universe into being. He explains why in the following viewpoint.

Consider the following questions while reading:

1. **What significant discovery did Arno Penzias and Robert Wilson make in 1965 at the Bell Laboratories?**
2. **According to Jastrow, why are astronomers "curiously upset" over the prospect of the universe having a beginning?**
3. **What does Jastrow say about the state of the universe before the Big Bang?**

When an astronomer writes about God, his colleagues assume he is either over the hill or going bonkers. In my case it should be understood from the start that I am an agnostic in religious matters. However, I am fascinated by some strange developments going on in astronomy — partly because of their religious implications and partly because of the peculiar reactions of my colleagues.

IN THE BEGINNING

The essence of the strange developments is that the Universe had, in some sense, a beginning — that it began at a certain moment in time, and under circumstances that seem to make it impossible — not just now, but *ever* — to find out what force or forces brought the world into being at that moment. Was it, as the Bible says, that

"Thou, Lord, in the beginning hast laid the foundations of the earth, and the heavens are the work of thine hands?"

No scientist can answer that question; we can never tell whether the Prime Mover willed the world into being, or the creative agent was one of the familiar forces of physics; for the astronomical evidence proves that the Universe was created twenty billion years ago in a fiery explosion, and in the searing heat of that first moment, all the evidence needed for a scientific study of the cause of the great explosion was melted down and destroyed.

This is the crux of the new story of Genesis. It has been familiar for years as the "Big Bang" theory, and has shared the limelight with other theories, especially the Steady State cosmology; but adverse evidence has led to the abandonment of the Steady State theory by nearly everyone, leaving the Big Bang theory exposed as the only adequate explanation of the facts.

AN EXPANDING UNIVERSE

The general scientific picture that leads to the Big Bang theory is well known. We have been aware for fifty years that we live in an expanding Universe, in which all the galaxies around us are moving apart from us and one another at enormous speeds. The Universe is blowing up before our eyes, as if we are witnessing the aftermath of a gigantic explosion. If we retrace the motions of the outward-moving galaxies backward in time, we find that they all come together, so to speak, fifteen or twenty billion years ago.

At that time all the matter in the Universe was packed into a dense mass, at temperatures of many trillions of degrees. The dazzling brilliance of the radiation in this dense, hot Universe must have been beyond description. The picture suggests the explosion of a cosmic hydrogen bomb. The instant in which the cosmic bomb exploded marked the birth of the Universe.

Now we see how the astronomical evidence leads to a biblical view of the origin of the world. The details differ, but the essential elements in the astronomical and biblical accounts of Genesis are the same: the chain of events leading to man commenced suddenly and sharply at a definite moment in time, in a flash of light and energy.

LIMITS OF SCIENCE

Of creation science cannot say anything at all. Scientific cosmology takes us to the place where philosophy and theology begin.

Stanley Jaki, Theologian and Physicist, Seton Hall University

---

PENZIAS AND WILSON

Some scientists are unhappy with the idea that the world began in this way. Until recently many of my colleagues preferred the Steady State theory, which holds that the Universe had no beginning and is eternal. But the latest evidence makes it almost certain that the Big Bang really did occur many millions of years ago. In 1965 Arno Penzias and Robert Wilson of the Bell Laboratories discovered that the earth is bathed in a faint glow of radiation coming from every direction in the heavens. The measurements showed that the earth itself could not be the origin of this radiation, nor could the radiation come from the direction of the moon, the sun, or any other particular object in the sky. The entire Universe seemed to be the source.

The two physicists were puzzled by their discovery. They were not thinking about the origin of the Universe, and they did not realize they had stumbled upon the answer to one of the cosmic mysteries. Scientists who believed in the theory of the Big Bang had long asserted that the Universe must have

Robert Jastrow

resembled a white-hot fireball in the very first moments after the Big Bang occurred. Gradually, as the Universe expanded and cooled, the fireball would have become less brilliant, but its radiation would have never disappeared entirely. It was the diffuse glow of this ancient radiation, dating back to the birth of the Universe, that Penzias and Wilson apparently discovered.*

A PUZZLING CONFLICT

No explanation other than the Big Bang has been found for the fireball radiation. The clincher, which has convinced almost the last doubting Thomas, is that the radiation discovered by Penzias and Wilson has exactly the pattern of wavelengths expected for the light and heat produced in a great explosion. Supporters of the Steady State theory have tried desperately to find an alternative explanation, but they have failed. At the present time, the Big Bang theory has no competitors.

Theologians generally are delighted with the proof that the Universe had a beginning, but astronomers are curiously upset. Their reactions provide an interesting demonstration of the response of the scientific mind — supposedly a very objective mind — when evidence uncovered by science itself leads to a conflict with the articles of faith in our profession. It turns out that the scientist behaves the way the rest of us do when our beliefs are in conflict with the evidence. We become irritated, we pretend the conflict does not exist, or we paper it over with meaningless phrases...

VIOLATION OF SCIENTIFIC FAITH

Scientists cannot bear the thought of a natural phenomenon which cannot be explained, even with unlimited time and money. There is a kind of religion in science; it is the religion of a person who believes there is order and harmony in the Universe, and every event can be explained in a rational way as the product of some previous event; every effect must have its cause; there is no First Cause. Einstein wrote, "The scientist is possessed by the sense of universal causation." This religious faith of the scientist is violated by the discovery that the world had a beginning under conditions in which the known laws of physics are not valid, and as a product of forces or circumstances we cannot discover. When that hap-

*Ralph Alpher and Robert Herman predicted the fireball radiation in 1948 but no one paid attention to their prediction. They were ahead of their time.

48

pens, the scientist has lost control. If he really examined the implications, he would be traumatized. As usual when faced with trauma, the mind reacts by ignoring the implications — in science this is known as "refusing to speculate" — or trivializing the origin of the world by calling it the Big Bang, as if the Universe were a firecracker.

AN UNANSWERABLE QUESTION

Consider the enormity of the problem. Science has proven that the Universe exploded into being at a certain moment. It asks, What cause produced this effect? Who or what put the matter and energy into the Universe? Was the Universe created out of nothing, or was it gathered together out of pre-existing materials? And science cannot answer these questions, because, according to the astronomers, in the first moments of its existence the Universe was compressed to an extraordinary degree, and consumed by the heat of a fire beyond human imagination. The shock of that instant must have destroyed every particle of evidence that could have yielded a clue to the cause of the great explosion. An entire world, rich in structure and history, may have existed before our Universe appeared, but if it did, science cannot tell what kind of world it was. A sound explanation may exist for the explosive birth of our Universe; but if it does, science cannot find out what the explanation is. The scientist's pursuit of the past ends in the moment of creation.

LESSON IN HUMILITY

If scientists have learned anything from the theologians, it is that they too must approach the mysteries of nature with awe - and humility.

Edward Tivnan, *Focus*, June/July, 1980

THE MOUNTAIN OF IGNORANCE

This is an exceedingly strange development, unexpected by all but the theologians. They have always accepted the word of the Bible: In the beginning God created heaven and earth. To which St. Augustine added, "Who can understand

"What do you mean, 'Big Bang Theory'?"

Hector Breeze. © Punch/Rothco.

this mystery or explain it to others?" It is unexpected because science has had such extraordinary success in tracing the chain of cause and effect backward in time. We have been able to connect the appearance of man on this planet to the crossing of the threshold of life, the manufacture of the chemical ingredients of life within stars that have long since expired, the formation of those stars out of the primal mists, and the expansion and cooling of the parent cloud of gases out of the cosmic fireball.

Now we would like to pursue that inquiry farther back in time, but the barrier to further progress seems insurmountable. It is not a matter of another year, another decade of work, another measurement, or another theory; at this moment it seems as though science will never be able to raise the curtain on the mystery of creation. For the scientist who has lived by his faith in the power of reason, the story ends like a bad dream. He has scaled the mountains of ignorance; he is about to conquer the highest peak; as he pulls himself over the final rock, he is greeted by a band of theologians who have been sitting there for centuries.

"Any real comparison between what the bible says and what the astronomer thinks shows us instantly that the two have virtually nothing in common."

God Is Not the Creator

Isaac Asimov

Isaac Asimov is probably the most prolific science writer in America today. He has written countless books and articles, both scientific and science fiction, for young and adult readers. Asimov experienced a strong reaction to Jastrow's *God and the Astronomers*. In the following viewpoint, he explains why the bible and astronomy have nothing in common and expresses doubt that even Jastrow "takes his own book very seriously."

Consider the following questions while reading:
1. **List some of the comparisons between the Bible and astronomical research outlined by Asimov.**
2. **According to Asimov, what three things might be happening to the Universe?**
3. **Do you feel that Asimov's criticism of Viewpoint One is valid? Why or why not?**

Isaac Asimov, "Do Scientists Believe in God?", *Gallery,* June, 1979. By permission of the author and of Gallery Magazine ©copyright 1979 by Montcalm Publishing Corp.

Some scientists are making their peace with theology. If we listen to them, they will tell us that science has only managed to find out, with a great deal of pain, suffering, storm, and strife, exactly what theologians knew all along.

A case in point is Robert Jastrow, an authentic professor of astronomy who has now written a book called *God and the Astronomers*. In it he explains that astronomers have discovered that the Universe began very suddenly and catastrophically in what is called a big bang and that they're upset about it.

The theologians, however, Jastrow says, are happy about it, because the Bible says that the Universe began very suddenly when god said, *Let there be light!*

Or, to put it in Jastrow's very own words: "For the scientist who has lived by his faith in the power of reason, the story ends like a bad dream. He has scaled the mountains of ignorance; he is about to conquer the highest peak; as he pulls himself over the final rock, he is greeted by a band of theologians who have been sitting there for centuries."

If I can read the English language, Jastrow is saying that astronomers were sure, to begin with, that the Bible was all wrong; that if the Bible said the Universe had a beginning, astronomers were sure the Universe had *no* beginning; that when they began to discover that the Universe *did* have a beginning, they were so unhappy at the Bible being right that they grew all downcast about their own discoveries.

NOTHING IN COMMON

Furthermore, if I can continue to read the English language, Jastrow is implying that since the Bible has all the answers — after all, the theologians have been sitting on the mountain peak for centuries — it has been a waste of time, money, and effort for astronomers to have been peering through their little spyglasses all this time.

Perhaps Jastrow, abandoning his "faith in the power of reason" (assuming he ever had it), will now abandon his science and pore over the Bible until he finds out what a quasar is, and whether the Universe is open or closed, and where black holes might exist — questions astronomers are working with now. Why should he waste his time in observatories?

But I don't think Jastrow will, because I don't really think he believes that all the answers are in the Bible — or that he takes his own book very seriously.

In the first place, any real comparison between what the Bible says and what the astronomer thinks shows us instantly that the two have virtually nothing in common. And here are some real comparisons:

ONE. The Bible says that the Earth was created at the same time as the Universe was *(In the beginning god created the heaven and the earth),* with the whole process taking six days. In fact, whereas the Earth was created at the very beginning of creation, the Sun, Moon, and stars were not created until the fourth day.

The astronomer, on the other hand, thinks the Universe was created 15 billion years ago and the Earth (together with the Sun and the Moon) was not created until a little less than five billion years ago. In other words, for ten billion years the Universe existed, full of stars, but without the Earth (or the Sun or the Moon).

ACCIDENTAL DETAILS

Genesis is not a book of science. It is accidental if some things agree in detail. I believe the heavens declare the glory of God only to people who've made a religious commitment.

Owen Gingerich, Historian–Astronomer, Harvard University

TWO. The Bible says that in the six days of creation, the whole job was finished. *(Thus the heavens and the earth were finished, and all the host of them. And on the seventh day god ended his work which he had made).*

The astronomer, on the other hand, thinks stars were being formed all through the 15 billion years since the Universe was created. In fact, stars are still being formed now, and planets and satellites along with them; and stars will continue being formed for billions of years to come.

Cover of *American Atheist* magazine, October, 1980. Reprinted with permission.

THREE. The Bible says that human beings were created on the sixth day of creation, so that the Earth was empty of human intelligence for five days only.

The biologist, on the other hand, thinks (and the astronomer does not disagree) the earliest beings that were even vaguely human didn't appear on the Earth until well over 4½ billion years after its creation.

FOUR. The Bible doesn't say when the creation took place, but the most popular view among the theologians on that mountain peak is that creation took place in 4004 B.C.

As I've said, the astronomer thinks creation took place 15 billion years ago.

FIVE. The Bible says the Universe was created through the word of god.

The astronomer, on the other hand, thinks the Universe was created through the operation of the blind, unchanging laws of nature — the same laws that are in operation today.

(Notice, by the way, that in these comparisons I say, "The Bible says..." but "The astronomer thinks..." That is because theologians are always certain in their conclusions and scientists are always tentative in theirs. That, too, is an important distinction.)

THEOLOGIANS ON THEIR BACKS

There are enormous differences, and it would be a very unusual astronomer who could imagine finding any theologians on *his* mountain peak. Where are the theologians who said that creation took place 15 billion years ago? That the Earth was formed ten billion years later? That human beings appeared 4½ billion years later still?

Some theologians may be willing to believe this *now*, but that would only be because scientists showed them the mountain peak and carried them up there.

So what the devil is Jastrow talking about? Where is the similarity between the book of Genesis and astronomical conclusions?

One thing. One thing only.

The Bible says the Universe had a beginning. The astronomer thinks the Universe had a beginning.

That's all.

But even this similarity is not significant, because it represents a *conclusion*, and conclusions are cheap. *Anyone* can reach a conclusion — the theologian, the astronomer, the shoeshine boy down the street.

Anyone can reach a conclusion in any way — by guessing it, by experiencing a gut feeling about it, by dreaming it, by copying it, by tossing a coin over it.

And no matter who reaches a conclusion, and no matter how he manages to do it, he may be right, provided there are a sharply limited number of possible conclusions. If eight horses are running a race, you might bet on a particular horse because the jockey is wearing your favorite colors or because the horse looks like your Aunt Hortense — and you may win just the same.

If two men are boxing for the championship and you toss a coin to pick your bet, you have one chance in two of being right — even if the fight is rigged.

IRRELEVANT TO SCIENCE

That first instant of creation is not relevant as long as we do not have the laws to begin to understand it. It is a question for philosophers and religionists, not for scientists.

Harvey Tananbaum, X–ray astronomer, Harvard–Smithsonian Astrophysical Laboratory

---

THREE CHOICES

How does this apply to the astronomical and theological view of the Universe? Well, we're dealing with something in which there are a sharply limited number of conclusions — more than a two-man prizefight, but fewer than an eight-animal horserace. There are, after all, just three things that might be happening to the Universe in the long run:

A. The Universe may be unchanging, on the whole, and therefore have neither a beginning nor an end — like a fountain, which, although individual water drops rise and fall, maintains its overall shape indefinitely.

B. The Universe may be changing progressively; that is, in one direction only, and may therefore have a distinct beginning and a different end — like a person, who is born, grows older (never younger), and eventually dies.

C. The Universe may be changing cyclicly, back and forth, and therefore have an end that is at the beginning, so that the process starts over endlessly — like the seasons, which progress from spring, through summer, fall, and winter, but then return to spring again, so that the process starts over...

QUESTIONS NO THEOLOGIAN CAN ANSWER

What counts is *not* that astronomers are currently of the opinion that there was once a big bang, in which an enormously concentrated "cosmic egg" that contained all the matter there is exploded with unimaginably catastrophic intensity to form the Universe. What counts is the long chain of investigation that led to the observation of the isotropic radio wave background (shortwave radio waves that reach Earth faintly, and equally, from all directions) that supports that opinion.

So when the astronomer climbs the mountain, it is irrelevant whether theologians are sitting at the peak or not, if they have not *climbed* the mountain.

As a matter of fact, the mountain *peak* is no mountain peak; it is merely another crossroad. The astronomer will continue to climb. Jastrow seems to think the search has come to an end and there is nothing more for astronomers to find. There occasionally have been scientists who thought the search was all over. They are frequently quoted today, because scientists like a good laugh.

What was the cosmic egg and how did it come to explode at a particular moment in time? How did it form? Was there something before the big bang? Will the results of the explosion make themselves felt forever, or will the exploding fragments at some time begin to come together again? Will the cosmic egg form again and will there be another big bang? Is it alter-

UNCHANGING UNIVERSE

The Universe may be unchanging, on the whole, and therefore have neither a beginning nor an end — like a fountain, which, although individual water drops rise and fall, maintains its overall shape indefinitely.

Isaac Asimov

native C that is the true explanation of the Universe? — these are only some of the infinite number of questions that those astronomers who are not convinced it is all over are interested in. In their search they may eventually reach new and better conclusions, find new and higher mountain peaks, and no doubt, find on each peak guessers and dreamers who have been sitting there for ages and will continue to sit there. And the scientists will pass by on a road that, it seems possible, will never reach an end, but will provide such interesting scenery *en route* that this, by itself, gives meaning to life and mind and thought.

"The only satisfactory explanation is that there is a personal creator behind it all."

God is the Creator

Michael Cassidy

Michael Cassidy is a native of South Africa and president of Africa Enterprise, an interdenominational, interracial and international evangelistic team. He received his M.A. at Cambridge University, England, and his Master of Divinity at Fuller Theological Seminary, Pasadena, California. The author of a weekly syndicated newspaper column, "Window on the Word," Mr. Cassidy has written several books including *Where Are You Taking The World Anyway?* In the following viewpoint, he attempts to illustrate why the design and order inherent in the universe signifies the existence of a Creator God.

Consider the following questions while reading:
1. **What are the three answers the author gives to the question of "chance or design?"**
2. **What four factors does the author feel must be embraced while attempting to answer the question of "chance or design?"**
3. **What is your reaction to the author's arguments?**

Taken from *Christianity for the Open-Minded* by Michael Cassidy. ©1978 by Inter-Varsity Christian Fellowship of the USA and used by permission of Inter-Varsity Press.

CHANCE OR DESIGN?

Is the universe the product of impersonal energy, plus time, plus chance or is it the creation of an infinite, personal God? At no point can we escape the fact that we are here and are indeed living on a dot in space and revolving around a dangerously hot star which is part of one galaxy in ten billion. This is the reality around us. Small wonder that Fred Hoyle, the great British astronomer, should say, "The universe being what it is, the creation issue simply cannot be dodged." So then, chance or design? That is the question.

THREE ANSWERS

There seem to be three kinds of answer to this question. First, the agnostic view says we do not and cannot know the answer. Second, the "labeling solution" attaches a name (for example, *evolution* or *nature*, which are really other names for chance) to a process which has been discerned, and leaves it at that. Unfortunately, to name a process is not to explain it or account for setting the stage so the process could happen at all. Third, Christianity says that the only satisfactory explanation is that there is a personal Creator behind it all.

PATTERN, CAUSE, EFFECT

In seeking to decide which view to embrace, the inquirer needs to consider the following factors: (1) The universe seems to possess a unity and a regularity. It is not random, chaotic or unpredictable. Does this not require explanation? (2) There are clear evidences of pattern and design. Mechanisms such as the human eye or ear do not cease to astonish us. Looking up the telescope or down the microscope, we are left in wonder and awe at what we see. Is this all due to irrational chance? (3) In the midst of what seems to be an impersonal universe, mind, personality and self–consciousness have emerged. Can an impersonal, mindless cause explain a personal, "mindful" effect? (4) There is a mysterious thing called beauty, and we are creatures who apprehend it. Is this subjective nonsense? Or are we recognizing a quality in creation and a faculty in ourselves, which defies explanation in purely scientific terms?

My point in all this is that we are faced with a reality which seems to require explanation in terms of mind and not simply in terms of matter put into motion by random gaseous explosions in the infinite recesses of time.

NO ACCIDENT

When you get out there a quarter of a million miles away from home, you look at earth with a little different perspective. The earth looks big and beautiful and blue and white, and you can see from the antarctic to the north pole and the continental shores. The earth looks so perfect. There are no strings to hold it up. No fulcrum upon which it rests. You think of the infinity of space and the infinity of time... I didn't see God. But I am convinced of God by the order out in space. I know it didn't happen by accident.

Eugene A. Cernan, Apollo 17 astronaut

The Apollo II lunar module. Courtesy of the National Aeronautics and Space Administration (NASA).

PLAIN TRUTH

Human beings can be explained physically in terms of chemical composition, but that is not all there is to know about them. Likewise the universe may be explicable up to a point in terms of physics and chemistry, but is it not also possessed of attributes which point to realities of another kind? If our minds can comprehend it in some measure and unravel it, is that not additional evidence that mind is meeting mind? After all, the scientist does not put truth into the universe. He simply uncovers or discovers truth which is already there. The Christian says it is the truth of the Creator God, not of impersonal and random chance.

What do you think?

DISTINGUISHING BETWEEN BIAS AND REASON

The subjects of science and religion often generate great emotional responses in people. This is especially true when the two are compared as avenues of truth. It seems obvious that when dealing with such highly controversial subjects, many will allow their feelings to dominate their powers of reason. Thus, one of the most important critical thinking skills is the ability to distinguish between opinions based upon emotion or bias and conclusions based upon a rational consideration of the facts.

PART I

Instructions

Some of the following statements have been taken from the viewpoints in this book and some have other origins. Consider each statement carefully. Mark *R* for any statement you feel is based on reason and a rational consideration of the facts. Mark *B* for any statement you believe is based on bias, prejudice or emotion. Mark *I* for any statement you think is impossible to judge. Then discuss and compare your judgements with other class members.

> R = A Statement Based On Reason
> B = A Statement Based On Bias
> I = A Statement Impossible To Judge

_____ 1. The existence of God cannot be proven. It is based upon faith alone.

_____ 2. Because of the beauty and order of the universe, there must have been a Divine Creator.

_____ 3. Atheism hates ignorance. So does science. It is natural that they should flourish together.

_____ 4. There is no scientific reason why God cannot retain the same position in our modern world that He held before we began probing His creation with the telescope and cyclotron.

_____ 5. The only way that we can know about the origin of things is by guesswork or divine revelation. Here creationists have the decided advantage.

_____ 6. Scientists cannot disprove that God is the Creator nor can theologians prove that He is.

_____ 7. If the human race is to advance technologically, scientists should ignore the question of ethics.

_____ 8. Just because a new technology can be done, it doesn't necessarily mean that it should be done.

_____ 9. The idea of creation should not be rejected because it can be associated with religion; rather it should be judged by how well it can be fitted to the known facts.

_____ 10. Far from taking God out of the universe, the theory of evolution gives us a more sublime conception of God's creative act. He operates through the laws of nature that He has established.

_____ 11. To say that a person is wrong to bring a child into the world differently than you would do it is arrogant.

_____ 12. Evolution best explains the origin and development of life.

PART II

Instructions

STEP 1

The class should break into groups of four to six students.

STEP 2

Each small group should try to locate four statements in this book. Two of the statements should display an author's bias and two should be based upon reason.

STEP 3

Each group should choose a student to record its statements.

STEP 4

The class should discuss and compare the small groups' statements.

BIBLIOGRAPHY

The editors have compiled the following list of periodical articles which deal with the subject matter of this chapter. The majority of periodicals listed are available in most school and public libraries.

H. O. J. Brown

Only God Satisfies the Complexities of the Cosmos, **Christianity Today,** December 12, 1980, p. 76.

N. Calder

Key to the Universe, **Science Digest,** June, 1977, p. 58.

Robert A. Ginskey

God and the Astronomers, **The Plain Truth,** January, 1979, p. 2.

C. D. Linton

Rage for Chaos, **Christianity Today,** May 6, 1977, p. 22.

J. Marsh

Creation According to Cosmology, **Commentary,** October, 1977, p. 65.

Lance Morrow

In the Beginning: God and Science, **Time,** February 5, 1979, p. 149.

William J. O'Malley

Carl Sagan's Gospel of Scientism, **America,** February 7, 1981, p. 95.

M. Rees

Unfolding Universe: The 13,000,000,000-Year Bank, **Current,** February, 1977, p. 51.

Carl Sagan

Reflections on a Grain of Salt: Can We Know the Universe?, **Science Digest,** July, 1979, p. 8.

Ralph B. Shirley

The Big Bang Theory and Creation, **The American Atheist,** December, 1980, p. 14.

Chapter

3

science and religion

How Did
Life
Originate?

Which Garden of Eden?

C. CLEARY

"The only sound way to teach biology as a scientific discipline... is to emphasize evolution as a basic explanation for origins."

Evolution Best Explains Life's Origins

G. Ledyard Stebbins

G. Ledyard Stebbins (Ph.D. Harvard, 1931) is Professor Emeritus of Genetics at the University of California, Davis. The winner of numerous scientific awards including the National Medal of Science (1979–1980), he is a member of the National Academy of Sciences and was past President of the Society for the Study of Evolution. Dr. Stebbins is a prolific author who has written over 250 scientific papers and nine books, the most recent being *Molecules to Humanity, A Panorama of Evolution.* In the following viewpoint, Dr. Stebbins explains why he believes that evolution is the only valid explanation for the origins of and changes in life forms.

Consider the following questions while reading:
1. **How does the author differentiate scientists from creationists?**
2. **What are two of the most commonly raised objections to modern evolutionary theory? How does the author deal with these objections?**

G. Ledyard Stebbins, "Evolution as the Central Theme of Biology", *Biological Sciences Curriculum Newsletter,* No. 49, November, 1972. Reprinted with permission of the author.

The great majority of life scientists now agree that there is only one central theme about which all the facts about the millions of diverse kinds of organisms can be arranged. This is the generally recognized theory that modern species of animals, plants, and microorganisms are all descended from a continuous line of ancestors that stretches back billions of years to the time when life first appeared upon the earth. They have evolved from these ancestors at different times, at different rates, and in different directions. Biologists who know the facts regard the probability that evolution has occurred as about equal to the near certainty that in the past, before written records existed that modern men can read directly, men had formed great empires such as those of ancient Egypt, Sumer, Babylon, and Crete. The evidence for the origin of major groups or distinctive kinds of organisms, one from the other, is of the same kind and equally strong as the evidence which has enabled archeologists to reconstruct the civilizations of these ancient empires.

CONTRARY TO SCIENCE

Creationists insist that the universe is only a few thousand years old, and that all life forms appeared on earth within a few days. Striking evidence to the contrary comes from almost every branch of science.

Robert J. Schadewald, *Minneapolis Star,* April 4, 1979

SPECIAL CREATION NOT SCIENTIFIC

The only alternative to evolution that is seriously proposed to explain the origin of different kinds of animals, plants, and mankind is special creation. Scientists cannot deal with this alternative, since it is not science. Scientists build and test hypotheses; the "creationists" would have us accept special creation on faith, if they have, to their satisfaction, gathered enough "evidence" to cause them to doubt the occurrence of evolution. The belief in special creation is untestable. Those who advocate its inclusion in the science curricula of our public schools do not permit scientists to criticize it or examine it. One cannot question the ability or the way in which a supreme being could have created the millions of different kinds of living organisms that exist on the earth.

TWO COMMON OBJECTIONS TO EVOLUTION

Two of the objections which are most commonly raised by "creationists" to modern evolutionary theory are first, that transitional fossils between major groups of animals do not exist. This statement is erroneous. In a letter to me dated August 4, 1972, Professor A. S. Romer of Harvard, one of the world's leading paleontologists, has stated: "....over the course of the past century more and more transitional forms have been discovered. If we consider the group of vertebrates, in which we are all most specifically interested...for all higher groups transitions are definitely known." Another authority of equal eminence, Professor G. G. Simpson, states (letter of August 1, 1972): "Literally thousands of transitional forms are known, and more are discovered every year."

BEND THE FACTS

Fundamentalist creationism is not a science but a form of antiscience, whose more vocal practitioners, despite their master's and doctoral degrees in the sciences, play fast and loose with the facts of geology and biology.

Preston Cloud, *The Humanist*, January/February, 1977

Further support for the existence of many transitional forms comes from paleontologists J. T. Gregory, University of California, Berkeley; William Clemens of the same institution; Everett Olson of U. C. Los Angeles; and F. Crompton of Harvard. The fact must be emphasized that these scientists base their conclusions upon intimate first hand knowledge of the fossils themselves, while the recent claims that others have voiced saying that transitions do not exist are based only upon reading second hand and third hand sources.

A second objection made by the "creationists" to modern evolutionary theory is that biologists cannot explain the origin of life. This statement is also erroneous. Several experiments have shown that the basic molecules of which living organisms consist can be synthesized from compounds that were almost certainly present on the primeval earth. The methods of synthesis imitate processes that could very probably have taken place when a terrestrial environment favorable for life first appeared. The arrangement of these molecules into functional systems that were self-reproducing, and their evolution finally into the first cellular organisms, can be explained by processes of chemical mutation, recombination, and natural selection similar to the processes that have been experimentally demonstrated to be responsible for change of micro-evolutionary order in contemporary organisms. Experiments by biochemists have shown that these processes can operate to produce progressive change in acellular systems similar to the processes that are postulated to have preceded the development of cellular forms of life.

At present, several well financed research laboratories in the United States are investigating the chemical basis of the origin of life.

The only way to teach biology as a scientific discipline in the contemporary modern world is to emphasize evolution as a basic explanation for origins.

"We don't object to the teaching of Darwinism, but as creationists, we do object to having it presented as a factual science."

Reprinted from *National Review* magazine, 150 E. 35 St., New York, NY 10016.

"Creation offers a more attractive philosophical alternative to evolution."

Divine Creation Best Explains Life's Origins

Jordan Lorence

Scientific creationists attempt to use the instruments of science to prove their arguments for divine creation and against evolution (See Viewpoint 4 in this chapter.) In the following viewpoint, however, Jordan Lorence relies upon logic, rather than science, to try to disprove the tenet of evolution. Mr. Lorence is a law student at the University of Minnesota and a former reporter for the *Minnesota Daily*.

Consider the following questions while reading:

1. **How does the author use the forest analogy to show that it requires less faith to believe in creation than in evolution?**
2. **According to the author, what are the three important conclusions asserted by the theory of evolution? What three questions does Lorence ask to challenge these conclusions?**
3. **The author relies upon logic, rather than scientific evidence, to disprove evolution. Did you find his arguments strong or weak? Explain your answer.**

Jordan Lorence, "Creation Theory Deserves Hearing", *Minnesota Daily*, February 20, 1980.

The creation theory of life's beginnings deserves a fair hearing.

To many who were raised on the theory of evolution, creation sounds like little more than unscientific, medieval superstition.

But today, many scientists have marshalled evidence to show that the theory of creation is a scientifically plausible alternative to evolution.

EVOLUTION: A SUPERSTITION

The world has traded in one superstition for another. The iron hand of medieval theologians has been replaced by the educated fist of evolutionists.

William F. Dankenbring, *Plain Truth,* June, 1973

EVOLUTION'S SHORTCOMINGS

I am not a scientist. I cannot adequately evaluate all the scientific evidence on both sides. But to me, evolution suffers some major logical and philosophical shortcomings that the theory of creation does not share.

Evolution is the theory that all life gradually developed by chance from a single cell, which developed earlier from non-living matter. The theory of creation states that all forms of life came into existence suddenly by the work of a supernatural creator.

Both evolution and creation are theories. No one was around when the universe began, so no one can say for certain what happened back then. All scientists can do is sift through the evidence and make guesses about what happened long ago.

My first problem with evolution is that it attributes the existence of complex forms of life to such simple things as "chance" and "survival of the fittest." To say that the human brain was fashioned by an intelligent creator makes more sense to me than saying it evolved by chance, even allowing for billions of years of mutants and change.

Apply this to a different setting. Imagine two people are walking through a forest. One is a creationist, the other an evolutionist. They spy a wristwatch lying on the trail. The creationist says, "someone must have dropped this here." The evolutionist says, "millions of years ago, rainwater from the mountains brought metal ores down to this trail. They formed into a crude watchband and set of hands. Then a bolt of lightning hit the randomly-formed battery and started the watch ticking."

Which hiker gives the more plausible story about the watch? Faced with the intricate forms of life on this planet, I think it takes more "faith" to believe it all evolved by chance than to believe a master designer created it.

Let me state this another way. A system built on chance or random selection, overwhelmingly results in chaos and disorder. Only beings with a creative intelligence can conceive and make form and order. When I see a building in a city, I attribute it to the creative powers of its architect and workmen. When I see a massive pile of bricks in the next lot, I attribute that to the random collisions of a wrecking ball. When I dump a basket of laundry on my bed, the socks and underwear never come out neatly folded, unless I've done it myself beforehand.

EVOLUTION'S THREE CONCLUSIONS

Another problem I have with the theory of evolution is that it asserts three incredibly important conclusions, yet offers little evidence to support or explain them. The three conclusions are: first, that something came out of nothing; second, that life came out of non-life; and third, that human life came out of non-human life.

If there is no creator, why is there something rather than nothing? If there is no creator, where did evolution's raw materials come from? If they have always existed, where is the proof?

Also, to think that the same chemicals that form rocks could somehow turn into amoebas, and then fish, and then mammals, and then man, staggers the imagination, even granting billions of years for all of this to occur. What

"Now children I realize Great Grandfather may seem a little strange to you, but..."

changed non-living chemicals into life? What changed animals into humans? To simply say it "happened" merely states a conclusion and does not adequately answer the question.

EVOLUTION AND HUMAN DIGNITY

Another major problem I see with evolution is that it strips human beings of their significance and dignity. If a man is merely a random product of chance evolution, then of what value are love, or brotherhood, or self-sacrifice for others? They are all a cruel joke, for the only reality is survival of the fittest.

Creation offers a more attractive philosophical alternative to evolution. We humans are significant beings, capable of meaningful feelings, thoughts and relationships because we are made in the image of the intelligent creator. To fight for human rights is to fight for the rights of those made in the image of God, not the rights of insignificant lumps that will quickly disappear into the gut of impersonal evolutionary forces. Simply put, man means something in creation, he means nothing in evolution.

Let creation have a fair hearing. We will then be able to critically scrutinize and compare the evidence for the two theories. Also, we may find a theory of life's beginnings that gives significance and meaning to our lives as human beings.

"Evolution theory is a natural process; a scientific framework supported by facts, experience, and reason."

Creationism Is No Alternative To Evolution

H. James Birx

Free Inquiry is a new humanist publication which, according to a front page editorial in its first issue, is intent upon defining and defending "the positions of freedom and secularism in the contemporary world." The following viewpoint by H. James Birx, chairman of the sociology and anthropology department, Canisius College, Buffalo, appeared in that first issue. In it, the author offers some background to the Creation/Evolution Controversy and then attempts to explain why "special creationism is irrational in principle and, therefore, not admissible as scientific doctrine."

Consider the following questions while reading:
1. **According to Birx, how does evolution theory explain the appearence of new species of plants and animals?**
2. **The author offers several reasons for rejecting creationism as an explanation for the origin of species. List them.**

J. James Birx, "The Creation/Evolution Controversy", *Free Inquiry*, Winter, 1980/1981. ©1980 by *Free Inquiry*, Box 5, Central Park Station, Buffalo, New York 14215. Reprinted with permission.

Once again the scientific theory of biological evolution has come under scathing criticisms by the special creationists, especially the fundamentalist movement. Even after the Huxley–Wilberforce debate (1860) and the John Scopes trial (1925), the evolution framework continues to be challenged or rejected by orthodox religions and philosophies.

Given the strong differences today in commitments to religious faith or science, the ongoing controversy between the Bible and evolution is perhaps unavoidable. A critical examination of the arguments given to refute the claims of the evolution viewpoint is required. Such a serious investigation shows the creationist/fundamentalist position to be untenable as a scientific theory.

Proponents claim that the creationist theory is scientific, but they actually disregard any facts that contradict their religious viewpoint. More alarming, they are even insisting that special creationism be taught on an equal basis with the evolution theory in science courses in public schools (especially in biology classes). . .

This movement is primarily the result of efforts from the Institute for Creation Research, in San Diego. It is made up of chemists and engineers, but few if any biologists. Seven staff scientists all have doctoral degrees and spend most of their time promoting creationism on college campuses and writing books advocating their position (the texts are published by the Creation–Life Publishers, also in San Diego).

THE CASE FOR EVOLUTION

What is the case for evolutionism?
Influenced by Lyell and Malthus, both Darwin and Wallace argued for biological evolution by means of natural selection or the "survival of the fittest." In *On the Origin of Species* (1859) and *The Descent of Man* (1871), Darwin presented a naturalistic–mechanistic explanation for organic evolution which still remains the essential foundation of modern evolution theory. As a science, modern evolution biology is a complex system of ideas that explains similarities and differences among organisms within space and throughout earth history.

The evolutionist holds that new species of plants and animals have risen from earlier, different forms over vast periods of time. As a result of selective forces (especially the major explanatory principle of natural selection) and the chance appearance and accumulation of favorable slight variations or major mutations, some individuals in a population have an adaptive and survival advantage and therefore a reproductive advantage over others. These individuals are favored in the struggle to exist in a changing environment.

SCIENCE IS MOST RELIABLE

We believe the scientific method, though imperfect, is still the most reliable way of understanding the world. Hence, we look to the natural, biological, social and behavioral sciences for knowledge of the universe and man's place within it.

From: "A Secular Humanist Declaration," *Free Inquiry*, Winter, 1980/81

THE FUNDAMENTALISTS' VIEW

Appealing to biblical chronology, the Ussher–Lightfoot calculations held that God created the world in 4004 B.C. on October 23 at 9:00 A.M. Many fundamentalists still believe this account of creation to be true. They claim the earth is less than 6,000 years old and that every kind of plant and animal is fixed in an ordered nature (although they do acknowledge varieties within these fixed types).

These fundamentalists now refer to their religious view as "scientific creationism," while rejecting the tenets of organic evolution. Despite the separation of church and state, they demand that biology textbooks give equal attention to both the story of divine creation as presented in Genesis and the modern synthetic theory of biological evolution grounded in natural selection and genetic variability . . .

Yet, the Bible is not a valid scientific document. Special creationism is theology and not an empirical–logical explanation for the origin and history of life on this planet. As a religious view, it appeals to the supernatural and the authority of the Bible (not to mention that it is biased in excluding all other creation stories except the Judeo–Christian account).

Creationism is neither falsifiable nor verifiable in principle. It ignores the established facts of the evolutionary sciences (e.g., the evidence from historical geology, comparative paleontology, and prehistoric archaeology, as well as the recent advances in genetic research and the use of absolute dating techniques.) Creationism consistently misrepresents the evolution theory and ultimately breaks down under rigorous logical scrutiny.

SPECIAL CREATIONISM IS IRRATIONAL

Special creationism is irrational in principle and, therefore, not admissable as a scientific doctrine. To suggest that scientific investigation and explanation for the rock and fossil and artifact records support a literal interpretation of Genesis is ludicrous; such a view ignores both facts and logic in favor of biblical authority and religious assumptions.

In sharp contrast, the evolution model has not been refuted by either empirical tests or the principle of falsifiability. Evolution remains a meaningful theory, in its explanation of evidence and prediction of events in modern biology and physical anthropology.

WESTERN RELIGIONS ACCEPT EVOLUTION

Most Western religions do, in fact, accept the evolution theory as the creative process throughout natural history. God remains as the First Cause of the universe, if not also the Creator of only the common source or first forms of all life.

There is a crucial distinction between the scientific fact of evolution and the various interpretations of this natural process in the literature. Bold attempts to reconcile scientific evolution with religious beliefs have failed, being poor compromises grounded in obscurantism. The natural and supernatural are not compatible in terms of facts and logic . . .

Evolution theory is a natural process; a scientific framework supported by facts, experience, and reason. It is open to modifications and interpretations in light of new empirical evidence, rigorous reflection, and logical procedure.

Unlike the special creationist or fundamentalist, the evolutionist as naturalist and humanist accepts the far-reaching implications of the evolutionary sciences. The planet Earth is not the center of reality, nor does man occupy a privileged position within natural history or the universe.

Although questions remain to be answered at this time, evolutionists continue to make progress through the ongoing and self-correcting method of scientific investigation. What is clearly needed is more science; the continued free inquiry into the origin and history of life on the earth.

"Creation theory does accommodate the available evidence as well as or better than evolution theory."

Creationism is the Best Alternative to Evolution

Harold G. Coffin

Harold G. Coffin is a member of the Geoscience Research Institute staff and professor of paleontology at Andrews University, Berrien Springs, Michigan. He has a doctorate in zoology from the University of Southern California (1955). A member of the American Association for the Advancement of Science and the Creation Research Society, Dr. Coffin has written or coauthored five books dealing mainly with evidences for creation. In the following viewpoint, he outlines what he believes to be convincing scientific evidence in support of the Creation theory.

Consider the following questions while reading:

1. **Compare the author's viewpoint to that of Stebbins (viewpoint one). What do both say regarding fossil evidence? Who do you support? Explain your answer.**
2. **What is the saltation theory? the "explosive evolution" theory?**
3. **List several facts that the author claims will be true of living things if the creation theory is correct.**

Harold G. Coffin, "Creationism: Is It a Viable Alternative to Evolution as a Theory of Origins?", *Liberty,* March/April, 1979. Reprinted by permission of the author from *Liberty,* a Magazine of Religious Freedom, ©1979 Review and Herald Publishing Association.

Harold G. Coffin

Many scientists and lay people are inclined to think that evolution theory is scientific but creation theory is not; that only evolution is supported by facts and open to study by the scientific method of observation and experimentation. Before examining creation theory to determine its validity as a viable theory of origins, let us see whether evolution really is scientific and supported by facts . . .

THE CARELESS CLAIMS OF EVOLUTIONISTS

Many careless claims concerning evolution (meaning major change from simple to complex) are published by individuals who know that only minor changes can be proved and who fail to distinguish between microevolution and macroevolution! Hereafter the word "evolution" will be used throughout this article to mean the general theory of evolution—macroevolution—unless otherwise indicated.

The general theory of evolution is contrary to some of the basic laws of science. Let me illustrate. In all recorded history, in all the experience of man, past and present, there has never once been a documented observation or laboratory experiment of the change of non-living matter into a living organism. Yet the *modus operandi* of science involves observation and experimentation. One of the most fundamental laws of biology is that life must come from life . . .

The theory of evolution requires gradual change from simple to complex, from one kind of organism to another. Here again, the total experience of man as a grower of crops, as a breeder of animals, and as a reproducing organism himself is contrary to such continuous change. Organisms do change—witness the many modern breeds of dogs, the new varieties of roses that appear regularly, and DDT-resistant strains of flies. But to insist that such minor changes accumulate into major differences across the boundaries separating basic kinds of organisms is an extrapolation not based on empirical evidence and contrary to another basic law of life— that offspring are like their parents. Dogs are still dogs, roses are still roses, and the resistant flies are very much pestiferous flies.

The theory of evolution stands only by contradicting two of the most fundamental laws of life—life begets life and like begets like.

NO CONNECTING LINES

The general theory of evolution also lacks evidence to support its most basic postulates. Let me illustrate this also. Since minor change (microevolution) is not the issue of concern (proponents of both creation and evolution theories recognize such transformations), we must look for evidences of major change from one basic kind to another. Most adults know that modern plants and animals fall into distinct groups or categories. We naturally speak of dogs or horses or roses or lilies, and everyone who hears us knows what kinds of animals and plants we are referring to. If dogs merged gradually into the bear family and carrots into beets, how could we let anyone know clearly what animal or plant we meant? If all modern animals and plants have evolved from common ancestors through many long series of gradual transitions, there should be evidence among the living fauna and flora for a continuous chain of life. Not just one link but many links—indeed, whole portions—are missing from the presumed evolutionary chain.

Some argue that there is no continuum now because many connecting forms (missing links) of life have become extinct or have not been preserved. Fossils provide a record of the past, pages out of nature's history book, and will constitute the ultimate court of appeal. If evolution has taken place, fossils will reveal it; if it has not taken place, they will refute it. The study of fossils has clearly shown a conspicuous absence of connecting links. Darwin was aware of this problem and stated that perhaps the greatest argument against his theory was the absence of intermediate or connecting forms between the major categories . . .

Lack of ancestors and connecting links has been so apparent that various secondary theories have been developed to account for it. The saltation theory says that evolution has progressed by major jumps and therefore no gradual transitions can be found—almost as though a reptile laid an egg that hatched a bird. No such unusual sudden changes can be seen in the many mutations that have been studied. Such "hopeful monsters" are unknown. The saltation theory represents a desperate attempt to accommodate the facts without accepting creation.

A DECIDED ADVANTAGE

The only way that we can know about the origin of things is by guesswork or divine revelation. Here creationists have the decided advantage.

J. W. Jepson, *The Christian Reader*, September/October, 1978

THE EXPLOSIVE EVOLUTION THEORY

Another theory proposes "explosive evolution" early in the history of life, and a relatively steady state since that time. Although such a theory does fit the fossil evidence better, few scientists accept it. Why was evolution rapid 600 million or more years ago but unable to cross the boundaries separating major types since that time? Gradual evolution by numerous minor steps since the beginning is the dominant view among evolutionists. Creationists would substitute "creation" for "explosive evolution."

THE PUNCTUATED EQUILIBRIA THEORY

A more recent proposal suggests that the actual process of evolution takes place along the fringes of a population where minor changes and variations are more likely to be isolated from the rest of the population. These would undergo rapid evolution until stability was achieved; then the entire population would be replaced by this new stable but more fit descendant (punctuated equilibria). Because the evolving would proceed by spurts among small peripheral populations, little fossil evidence would be preserved in the sediments . . .

"Saltation," "explosive evolution," "hopeful monsters," "punctuated equilibria"—these theories and others not mentioned would never have arisen if the need did not exist to explain the glaring inconsistencies between the fossil record and the basic requirements of the theory of evolution . . .

DESIGN IN LIVING

Design in living things has long been used as a strong argument for creation and against evolution. Darwin once said that the contemplation of the human eye gave him a cold shudder.

Anthropologists may find arrowheads, scrapers, or other simple man–made objects. Scrapers consisting of a stone with one sharp edge may be difficult to distinguish from a naturally broken stone. By carefully noting the cutting edge, the regular sequence of the pieces that were broken off, or the patterns of wear, the investigator may conclude that human design was involved and that this crude rock is a tool.

When the fantastic design of a rose or a bat or even a single cell is examined, no such conclusion is reached. The organism came about by the fortuitous operation of the laws of chance! To use design as an argument for identifying man-made objects but to refuse to use it for objects not made by man must be an example of anthropocentric ego.

The average individual feels a need to know and believe something about origins. Those who do not wish to start with a Creator have no alternative but to turn to some theory involving spontaneous generation. Each person is free to make his choice. Neither belief, spontaneous generation or creation, is true science, because there is no way to observe what happened at the beginning; no way to repeat in the laboratory the events that began life on earth. The study of origins belongs in the realm of philosophy.

CREATION IS MORE RATIONAL

Ultimately, acceptance of either creation or evolution involves a faith commitment, but creationists maintain that the scientific evidence that is available provides a much more rational basis for belief in creation than for belief in evolution.

Duane T. Gish, *The Humanist,* November/December, 1977

VALIDATING THE CREATION THEORY

One of the measures of the value of a theory is its ability to anticipate research results. On the basis of the Creation theory, what would we expect in the realm of living things and their historical records (fossils)?

1. Creation theory predicts that living organisms are too intricate in design and too complex in function to be the product of random molecular combinations and mutations . . .

2. Creation theory suggests that distinct and complex organisms would appear without ancestors in the record of past life preserved in the earth as fossils . . .

3. Creation theory suggests that complex organisms would remain distinct (lack of connecting links) during the time life has existed upon the earth . . .

4. Creation theory expects that organisms would resist change into new and different basic kinds by modern breeding or genetic experimentation . . .

5. Creation theory predicts that such change as has been experienced by organisms would not bridge basic taxonomic units such as families and higher categories . . .

6. Creation theory expects that mutations (considered the main driving force of evolution) and microevolutionary changes often would be neutral, harmful, or degenerative . . .

7. Creation theory predicts that though some ancient organisms would become extinct, all the basic kinds of modern living organisms would be represented in the fossil record by similar ancestors . . .

8. Creation theory predicts that basic categories of plants and animals would be widely distributed at their first appearance in the fossil record . . .

These eight expectations that cover both ancient and modern organisms reveal that creation theory does accommodate the available evidence as well as or better than evolution theory . . .

Since neither creation theory nor evolution theory is true science, we cannot make a decision on the basis of which one is science and which one is not. We must determine which theory is best supported by the total range of available evidences at hand, and which theory is closest to the method of operation and results we have learned to expect of science.

I believe that creation is a viable alternative theory of origins. It accommodates the facts of science more adequately than does evolution and should be given fair and unprejudiced consideration when the problem of origins is being studied.*

* **Editor's note:** *The original article from which this excerpt was taken contained 32 footnoted references. Dr. Coffin, the author, recommends that the interested reader review the footnotes in* **Liberty** *magazine.*

"It is a mistake to try to use the Bible as a textbook on science."

Keep Divine Creation Out of the Classroom

Bevel Jones

Bevel Jones is Senior Minister at the First United Methodist Church, Athens, Georgia. A graduate of Emory University and a Master of Divinity from the Chandler School of Theology, Reverend Jones writes regularly for the *Wesleyan Christian Advocate* and is a weekly columnist for the *Banner Herald/Daily News* in Athens. In the following viewpoint, he explains why "I for one will insist that we leave the teaching of science to the public schools and the teaching of religion to...the churches."

Consider the following questions while reading:
1. **List some of the author's objections to the teaching of "scientific creationism" in public schools.**
2. **According to the author, what *should* be learned from the Bible?**
3. **Do you agree with the author? Why or why not?**

Bevel Jones, "Science, Religion and the Georgia Legislature".Copyright 1981, Christian Century Foundation. Reprinted by permission from the January 7–14, 1981 issue of *The Christian Century.*

A bill now pending in the Georgia legislature proposes that "scientific creationism" be taught in any public elementary or secondary school in Georgia whenever the theory of evolution is taught. "Scientific creationism" is the theory that all forms of life were created by God *ex nihilo* (out of nothing) and according to their own original separate and distinct kind or species. This view precludes any sort of evolutionary development between species and is based fundamentally on a literal interpretation of the first two chapters of Genesis. Its proponents cite scientific data to support the premise of divine creation; thus the term scientific creationism.

A CHILL WIND

To suggest that we give Genesis equal time with evolution is like giving Pope Urban's math equal time with Galileo's. The creationists are people for whom the Bible is the only textbook. They would leave a chill wind for our children to inherit.

Ellen Goodman, *Washington Post Writers Group*

REASONS FOR OPPOSITION

I am opposed to House Bill 690 on several grounds. First of all, it is a violation of constitutional strictures against established or government-sponsored religion. The advocates of this bill are obviously religious people, and their motives are not in question. What they seem to have forgotten is that separation of church and state is not merely for the freedom of secular society, but for the protection of religious liberty. Christianity, as a voluntary movement, must be guarded against government-supervised and -required programs of religion that may be intended to foster belief in the God of Judeo-Christian faith, but that in fact would serve to undermine God's influence . . .

Those seeking to legislate scientific creationism as subject matter in our schools are orthodox Christians. What will happen if devotees of other faiths, such as Unitarians, Baha'is, Jews, Muslims or Buddhists, seek to have their particular theology of creationism imposed upon the minds of our youth? They could teach a theory of divine creationism that would comply fully with the law but which would be far from the intent of those proposing the law.

OBJECTIONS TO THE BILL

There are varying interpretations of the Bible even among Christians. In any congregation one will find disagreement as to exactly what is meant by a given passage of Scripture.

Christians are now experiencing intense controversy over what is termed by the more conservative as "the battle for the Bible." We are seeing a renewal of the fundamentalist-modernist conflict that raged in this country in the 1920s and '30s. It will be exceedingly unfortunate if state legislatures add fuel to this fire! If we cannot agree among ourselves in churches and religious assemblies, are we to expect agreement on prescribed religious curricula in public schools?

Another objection to the bill is its assumption or implication that evolution is necessarily atheistic. The materials prepared for use in the classroom by creationists offer only two options: creationism and evolution — i.e., "for" or "against" God. There is no suggestion of a third alternative—for example, theistic evolution, or what philosophers call "creative evolution." House Bill 690 makes no allowance for the belief that evolution is a valid part of the way God creates . . .

It is a mistake to try to use the Bible as a textbook on science. The creation story is neither empirical science nor recorded history. It is a religious interpretation divinely inspired in a prescientific age. It is not a literal account reported by bystanders. Genesis 1, 2 and 3 are the product of that sense of the mystical, the transcendent, that which infuses all being with meaning, purpose and value. The biblical narrative of creation is the deepest poetry of the human spirit, reaching beyond the sensory perception of pure science. Far from being unreal, or untrue, it lays hold of reality that can only be perceived spiritually, and expressed in the language of story, parable or metaphor . . .

A FALSE PREMISE

Christian fundamentalists . . . are attempting to introduce their religious beliefs into classrooms by attempting to have them considered scientific.

William V. Mayer, *Liberty,* September/October, 1978

WHAT THE BIBLE TELLS US

The Bible and science are reconciled not by superimposing the Bible on scientific data or vice versa, but by letting each do its own thing: science explaining the *method* of creation; the Bible interpreting the *meaning* of creation. These are textual materials for separate and distinct curricula—not to be confused in the science class. Galileo was right when he insisted: "The Bible tells us how to go to heaven, not how the heavens go." Science is designed to tell us the *what* and *how* of natural phenomena; the Bible tells us *who* and *why*. Science is purely analytical and descriptive, saying in effect that as best we can determine, this is the way life came into being and the way it works now. It is not the province of natural scientists to draw religious conclusions. Neither is it the place of religionists to introduce or impose their convictions on data presented in a biology or geology class. They do have the right to use scientific data to support their faith judgments in a religious setting . . .

The Georgia proponents of scientific creationism are in an untenable position. Their proposed bill would do a disservice to both science and religion. The constitutional separation of church and state would prohibit the teaching of a religious understanding of creation in public schools. Furthermore, it would be impossible for well-intentioned Christians to agree on how creation should be taught in public schools. Should it be the literal interpretation of Genesis, or should it be presented as allegory or parable? I for one will insist that we leave the teaching of science to the public schools and the teaching of religion to the homes, the churches, the synagogues and the seminaries. Those who choose to take the book of Genesis literally are at liberty to do so. They have a perfect right to hold those views, and to express them as persuasively as they can. But they do not have the right to require science teachers to do so in the public schools.

6

"'Scientific creationism' can be taught without any reference to the Bible or to any other religious book."

Divine Creation Belongs in the Classroom

Robert E. Burns

Father Robert E. Burns is a Paulist priest who was ordained on February 5, 1939. He was active as a U.S. missionary and was once pastor of a rural church in Tennessee. Now retired, Father Burns was a popular national lecturer and authored countless articles on contemporary church issues. In the following viewpoint, he strongly supports the inclusion of "scientific creationism" in the curricula of public schools.

Consider the following questions while reading:

1. **What points does the author make regarding the Bible and the teaching of "scientific creationism" in public schools?**
2. **According to the author, what important questions regarding matter and life is science unable to answer?**
3. **What did Father Patrick O'Connell write concerning fossils and their relationship to the theory of evolution?**

Robert E. Burns, "Evolution – A Flawed Theory", *The Wanderer*, January 15, 1981. Reprinted with permission.

In the Georgia Legislature, a controversy is raging over whether "scientific creationism" should be taught in the public schools as an alternate theory to evolution.

To say that the theory of evolution is seriously flawed is the understatement of the age, and one does not have to be a scientist to recognize this fact. Yet evolution is pushed on students in our public schools. If a theory in medicine, aeronautics, or nuclear energy were similarly flawed, it would never be propagated.

THE BIBLE AND PUBLIC EDUCATION

Humanist science teachers oppose the teaching of "scientific creationism" because they regard it simply as an underhanded way of introducing the Bible into public education.

Yet "scientific creationism" can be taught without any reference to the Bible or to any other religious book. Studies of the laws of thermodynamics, the lack of evidence for mutation of species, and other scientific considerations support creationism.

The fact that creationism and the Bible arrive at the same conclusion as to the origin of this world and man's origin does not mean creationism is not scientific. After all, Plato and Aristotle by pure unaided reason came to a knowledge of God's existence, entirely apart from the Bible.

FITTING THE FACTS

The idea of creation should not be rejected because it can be associated with religion; rather, it should be judged by how well it can be fitted to the known facts.

Ariel A. Roth, *Liberty*, September/October, 1978

CONSIDERING BASIC QUESTIONS

In all the reports of the controversy in Georgia which I have heard on the radio, it seems to me that important basic questions are not being considered, or if they are, then media reports have been incomplete.

The questions are these: How do we explain the origin of matter? Matter is not external, because it is subject to constant change. Science can tell us nothing about the origin of matter, because science can deal only with existing matter. Again—how do we explain the origin of life? Whether we are considering vegetative life, sentient life, or human life, what was its origin in the first instance? A living object or creature contains something more than matter.

Further, how do we explain Homo sapiens? What was his origin? When and where did he first come into existence? Who was responsible for his existence? It is surely unthinkable that man could have been self-created.

Regardless of what age in human civilization we study, we find a marked essential difference between humans and all other species of life. Man alone of all God's creatures has rationality, the ability to think and choose. It has enabled man to take advantage of and build upon all the discoveries of the past, from the invention of the wheel and the discovery of fire in primitive days. No other creature on this earth has been able to do that. From all the evidence we have, dogs, cats, and horses carry on today the same way they did thousands of years ago. Yet men who live in high-rise condominiums do not live and conduct their business as did their cave man ancestors.

A CONSTITUTIONAL BASIS

The constitutional basis for the teaching of creationism lies both in the fact that it characterizes the beliefs of the people of just about all religious denominations, and it has a respectable scientific rationale.

George Soyenneger, *The Minneapolis Star,* March 14, 1979

For years we have been given the impression that all the evolutionists needed to prove their theory was to find the missing link. Archaeological research has brought forth various specimens of fossil remains, among them the Neanderthal man, the Piltdown man, the Peking man, and the Java man.

The late Fr. Patrick O'Connell, a recognized paleontologist (as well as a Catholic missionary) who spent some 40 years in China and knew Teilhard de Chardin personally, writes the following in his book *The Origin and Early History of Man* (p. 51): "Darwin himself admitted, and the same admission is made by his followers, that the only real evidence for the evolution of species is provided by fossils found in geological strata. The theory of evolution of species in general and of man in particular stands or falls by the fossil record. With regard to the question of the origin of the various species of living things, Darwin admitted that the evidence from the fossil remains, as it was known in his time, was against the theory; since his time no real progress has been made and the theory of the origin of species by gradual evolution, even in the modified form, remains unproved.

"The same principle applies to the theory of the evolution of man as to the evolution of species in general; the theory stands or falls by the evidence of the fossils; if genuine fossils of creatures intermediate between lower animal and man (which evolutionists call hominids) cannot be produced the case for human evolution collapses.

"For more than a century an intense search has been made for the fossil remains of hominids or missing links, and case after case of missing links has been put forth and has been afterwards rejected by responsible scientists. At the present time any person who has made a reasonable amount of research could challenge evolutionists to produce even one hominid or missing link that has been established with certainty."

7

"There is no intrinsic conflict between faith and science, between God the creator and evolutionary theory."

Theistic Evolution: A Third Alternative

Noel Riley

Sister Noel Riley, S.M. (Sisters of Mercy), teaches chemistry at Bishop Conaty Memorial High School, Los Angeles and is a member of the National Science Teachers' Association. She received her B.S. from San Francisco State University and her M.S. in chemistry from St. Louis University. A Du Pont Fellow (St. Louis University) and the recipient of three National Science Foundation Grants, Sister Riley was named one of the five outstanding science teachers of the San Francisco Bay area in the early 1950's. In the following viewpoint, she presents a possible "middle ground" between evolution without God and creationism without evolution.

Consider the following questions while reading:
1. **According to the author, if Genesis is not a book of science, what can be learned from it?**
2. **What analogy did the philosopher John O'Brien use to illustrate the possible hand of God in evolution? Do you agree with him? Why or why not?**
3. **Compare Sister Riley's viewpoint with viewpoints one and two or three and four in this chapter.**

Noel Riley, "Getting a Big Bang Out of Creation Theories", *Los Angeles Times*, March 10, 1981. Reprinted with permission of the author.

As one who wears two hats (or should I say a hat and a veil?), I am both angered and embarrassed when the origins of our universe are posed as a conflict between Genesis and evolution.

My hat? I have a master's degree in chemistry from St. Louis University, and have taught science and religion for more than 25 years. My veil? I am a Roman Catholic nun, a member of the Sisters of Mercy community. I firmly believe both in God and in evolution. My embarrassment? That "believers" should espouse a discredited fundamentalist view of creation, one that merits the scorn and ridicule of the scientific community. My anger? That there are some well-meaning people who confront the young with a false choice: *either* the biblical story of creation *or* evolutionary theory. My thesis? There is no intrinsic conflict between faith and science, between God the creator and evolutionary theory.

A MORE NOBLE VIEW

Ultimately, far from diminishing God, the evolutionary view is more noble . . . it underlines that our future direction is in our own free hands. We can evolve to higher stages . . . Or we can end it all prematurely.

Michael J. Farrell, *National Catholic Reporter*, March 13, 1981

GENESIS: AN ANCIENT BOOK

The book of Genesis was probably written between the 10th and 6th centuries B.C., much later than the oral traditions from which it sprang. What scientific knowledge did the inspired authors have? Only the knowledge of their time, which is the case with our generation, too. Was the science faulty? Certainly, unless you think the earth is flat, supported by a large turtle, with waters above and below, and kept in check by an enclosed firmament. Did the authors of Genesis intend to teach science? Certainly not. As Roman Catholic theologian Robert Bellarmine wrote some four centuries ago, "The Bible was written to show us how to go to heaven, not how the heavens go!" And, as St. Augustine observed in the 4th Century, "The gospels do not tell us that our Lord said, 'I will send you the Holy Ghost to teach you the course of the sun and moon'; we should endeavor to become Christians and not astronomers."

What Genesis does is relate — in simple, figurative language that could be understood by primitive people — the fundamental principles of salvation and the description then popular of the origins of the human race. Let us consider a few examples of the figurative language and the underlying message.

In Genesis, God is shown as a master craftsman fashioning the world in six days and resting on the seventh. Jews were required to keep the Sabbath as a day of rest, which is the most reasonable explanation for depicting God as resting on the Sabbath, too.

PERIODS OF TIME

The creation story uses a liturgical or mnemonic device, "God saw that it was good," to mark each great event of creation. Once it was considered necessary to think of "the days" as periods of time representing some thousands of years each. But the days can be understood simply as normal 24-hour periods, forming the literary framework of what was probably a prehistoric hymn. The use of this literary device had a practical purpose; it made memorization and recitation easier, for we are speaking of people who were largely illiterate.

The primitive cosmology of Genesis was used to teach that God created all things and to emphasize his transcendent power, and his love and concern for us. This view contrasted with the pagan epics, then widespread, in which creation was depicted as a struggle between the gods and the forces of chaos. The Hebrew people lived among idolaters and were surrounded by those who worshiped animals. The point of Genesis is that God is to be worshiped because it was He who created all these things.

And why is Eve described in Genesis as being formed from the side of Adam? To demonstrate that she is of the same nature as man, unlike animals, and does not deserve the subordinate position assigned women in pagan society.

The biblical story of creation has a religious purpose. It contains, but does not teach, errors. The evolutionary theory of creation, in contrast, has a scientific purpose, and the

GOD'S SUBLIME ACT

Far from taking God out of the universe, the theory of evolution gives us a more sublime conception of God's creative act. He operates through the laws of nature that He has established.

Noel Riley

search for truth is the province of astronomers, geologists, biologists and the like. These two purposes are distinct, and both offer truth to the human mind and heart. The mistake scientists make is drawing philosophical and religious inferences and deductions unwarranted by the scientific data; the mistake of religious leaders is using the Bible as a science textbook.

GOD AND EVOLUTION

At the time of the controversy over Galileo's theory of the universe, Bellarmine warned: "I say that if a real proof be found that the sun is fixed and does not revolve around the earth, but the earth around the sun, then it will be necessary, very carefully, to proceed to the explanation of the passages of Scripture which appear to be contrary, and we should rather say that we have misunderstood these than pronounce that to be false which is demonstrated."

Far from taking God out of the universe, the theory of evolution gives us a more sublime conception of God's creative act. He operates through the laws of nature that He has established. I am indebted to a contemporary philosopher John O'Brien for an analogy: Just as it shows more skill for a billiards player to get all eight balls in the pockets in one stroke, rather than eight (or nine!), so it is a loftier conception of God to imagine a single creative act, with secondary causes operative thereafter.

Today scientists trying to explain the origins of the universe favor the "big bang" theory. Does this contradict Genesis? Not at all. In fact, if I were tempted to embrace a discredited concordism, I would see in the first "big bang" the creative hand of God, and His lofty words: "Let there be light!"

DISTINGUISHING PRIMARY FROM SECONDARY SOURCES

A critical thinker must always question his or her sources of knowledge. One way to critically evaluate information is to be able to distinguish between PRIMARY SOURCES (a "firsthand" or eyewitness account from personal letters, documents, or speeches, etc.) and SECONDARY SOURCES (a "secondhand" account usually based upon a "firsthand" account and possibly appearing in newspapers, encyclopedias, or other similar types of publications). A diary about the Civil War written by a Civil War veteran is an example of a primary source. A history of the Civil War written many years after the war and relying, in part, upon that diary for information is an example of a secondary source. However, it must be noted that interpretation and/or point of view also play a role when dealing with primary and secondary sources. For example, the historian writing about the Civil War not only will quote from the veteran's diary but also will interpret it. That his or her interpretation may be incorrect is certainly a possibility. Even the diary or primary source must be questioned as to interpretation and point of view. The veteran may have been a militarist who stressed the glory of warfare rather than the human suffering involved.

Test your skill in evaluating sources by participating in the following exercise. Pretend that your teacher has asked you to write a research paper on the history of the conflict between science and religion. You are also asked to distinguish the primary sources you used from the secondary sources. Listed below are ten sources which may be useful in your research. Carefully evaluate each of them. First, place a P next to those descriptions you feel would serve as primary sources. Second, rank the primary sources assigning the number (1) to the most objective and accurate primary source, number (2) to the next accurate and so on until the ranking is finished. Repeat the entire procedure, this time placing an S next to those descriptions you feel would serve as secondary sources and then ranking them. Discuss and compare your evaluations with other class members.

P or S   **Rank in Importance**

_____   1. The court records of Galileo's trial before the Roman Inquisition.   _____

_____   2. Charles Darwin's book on evolution, *The Origin of Species.*   _____

_____   3. An editorial in a 19th century religious publication attacking Charles Darwin and the theory of evolution.   _____

_____   4. A book by an astronomer providing precise experimental data illustrating that the universe began with a "Big Bang."   _____

_____   5. A book by a journalist providing details of the major scientific discoveries of the 1980's.   _____

_____   6. The autobiography of John Scopes, the biology teacher who was tried and convicted in 1925 for teaching the theory of evolution in a Tennessee public school.   _____

_____   7. The biography of Clarence Darrow, the lawyer who defended John Scopes during the famous "monkey trial."   _____

_____   8. The research paper you are supposedly writing about the history of the conflict between science and religion.   _____

_____   9. A newspaper article by a famous theologian attacking all experimentation in the field of genetic engineering as a violation of God's laws.   _____

_____   10. Passages from the U.S. constitution dealing with the separation of church and state.   _____

BIBLIOGRAPHY

The editors have compiled the following list of periodical articles which deal with the subject matter of this chapter. The majority of periodicals listed are available in most school and public libraries.

Richard P. Aulie — *The Doctrine of Special Creation,* **Journal of the American Scientific Affiliation,** December, 1975, p. 164.

Tom Bethell — *Darwin's Mistake,* **Christianity Today,** June 17, 1977, p. 12.

G. Richard Bozarth — *The Meaning of Evolution,* **The American Atheist,** February, 1978, p. 19.

James H. Burtness — *Creation in Our Own Image: Christian Perspectives,* **The Christian Century,** September 20, 1978, p. 855.

James O. Buswell III — *Creationist Views on Human Origin,* **Christianity Today,** August 8, 1975, p. 4.

James L. Christian — *The Story of Life: A Four-Billion-Year Beginning,* **The Humanist,** May/June, 1976, p. 5.

The Christian Reader — *Evolution – The Grand Fantasy,* January/February, 1977, p. 53.

Preston Cloud — *Evolution Theory and Creation Mythology,* **The Humanist,** November/December, 1977, p. 53.

Laurie R. Godfrey — *Science and Evolution in the Public Eye,* **The Skeptical Inquirer,** Fall, 1979, p. 21.

Amadeus W. Grabau — *Sixty Years of Darwinism: A Look Backward and Forward,* **Natural History,** April, 1980, p. 123.

The Humanist — *A Statement Affirming Evolution as a Principle of Science,* January/February, 1977, p. 4.

Newsweek — *Is Man a Subtle Accident?,* November 3, 1980, p. 95.

Calvin Seerveld — *The Gospel of Creation,* **Christianity Today,** November 17, 1978, p. 18.

Clayton Steep — *Scientists in Quandry about Darwin,* **The Plain Truth,** February, 1981, p. 20.

Richard H. Utt — *Evolution Versus Creation in the Public Schools,* **Liberty,** January/February, 1980, p. 13.

David L. Willis — *Alternative Views of Evolution,* **Journal of the American Scientific Affiliation,** March, 1975, p. 2.

H. P. Zuidema — *Iowa Rules on Creationism in Schools,* **Liberty,** November/December, 1978, p. 21.

Chapter **4**

science and religion

Should Science Be Influenced By Religion?

Plain Truth magazine, March, 1980. Illustration by Randall Cole.

"Genetic research is indeed moral. In fact, the immorality would be neglect or prohibition of this research."

Genetic Engineering is Moral

John Deedy

A free-lance writer who resides in Rockport, Massachusetts, John Deedy has authored ten books, his most recent being *Apologies, Good friends...An Interim Biography of Daniel Berrigan, S.J.* Mr. Deedy is a graduate of Holy Cross College, Worcester, Massachusetts and received an M.A. from Trinity College, Dublin, Ireland. Prior to turning to free-lance writing, he worked as an editor for several publications including the prestigious *Commonweal*. In the following viewpoint, he takes the position that genetic research, inasmuch as it will benefit humankind, is a moral pursuit.

Consider the following questions while reading:

1. List some of the diseases the author feels genetic research may help eliminate.
2. How does the author deal with the fact that genetic scientists may be "playing God?"
3. Do you agree with the author's arguments? Why or why not?

John Deedy, "Genetic Research Is Moral", *U.S. Catholic,* October, 1979. Reprinted with permission from *U.S. Catholic,* published by Claretian Publications, 221 W. Madison St., Chicago, IL 60606.

Is genetic research moral? That's like asking if it is moral for a man or woman to fly because God didn't create either with wings. Genetic research is indeed moral. In fact, the immorality would be neglect or prohibition of this research.

GENETICS AND DISEASE

Let's get straight what we're talking about. Genetics: it's the science dealing with heredity, various and related biological processes, and the development of all forms of life, including the human. Why is it important to humankind? Because genetics is the key to life—and health. Genetics plays a part in sterility and fecundity. It plays a part in more than 500 diseases. A quarter-million children are born each year in the United States with birth defects, and 20 percent of these defects are traceable to genetic causes. Many of these birth defects could be eliminated through preconceptive genetic medicine, genetic engineering, and other scientific procedures of a genetic kind. Sickle-cell anemia needn't forever be a high-risk blood disorder for blacks, nor must Tay-Sachs, an ailment of the nervous system, be forever a problem for a large number of children of Jewish ancestry. Genetic research can get at the causes of single genetic problems such as these just as it can attack more complex polygenic problems like diabetes and chromosome disorders like Down's syndrome. But it needs room to research.

A BRIGHT TOMORROW

I believe that human genetics has the potential to bring us to a society in which the worst genetic diseases can be controlled, in which the susceptibility of individuals to damage by environmental agents has been defined, and in which every individual can choose that physical, occupational, and social environment which is best adapted to his/her natural endowments.

Arno G. Motulsky, M.D., *Science Digest,* August, 1979

HERE TO STAY

It has some. Genetic research is already at work on a host of scientific and medical challenges. Inevitably these involve procedures and techniques that are often morally and ethically controversial, such as artificial gestations, cloning, enovulation from storage banks, and experiments in the pre-selection of sex, to mention but a few. Like it or not, such experimentation is not going to come to a halt by and of itself, much less as a result of thunderbolts from chanceries, angry editorials in the religious press, or directives from the Department of Health Education and Welfare (unless the latter have the force of law). Genetic research is here to stay—and that's a good thing. I'm not arguing that genetic scientists should be given a *carte blanche* to do as they would across the broad spectrum of possibilities. There must be limits. But neither condemnation nor hand-wringing nor reactionary restraints are going to give us such limits. Nor should they. Genetic science is to be respected . . .

THE MORAL CONTEXT

Nothing should induce us to bring genetic research to a screeching halt. If some genetic research results in abuses and in biological developments we find offensive—well, maybe we have no other choice but to live with them. As always, the future demands risks—and sacrifices. Precious few human breakthroughs in knowledge and experience have been accomplished without some negative effects. In its early stages, surgery claimed many victims, but, thank God, no one outlawed operations on humans as a consequence. So far as genetic research is concerned, it seems immoral to consign a person to deafness or to epilepsy, to mention but two disorders, when genetic engineering can be advanced to sophisticated points where a defective gene locus can be replaced with a healthy one . . .

We must push ahead with genetic research, and at the same time we must evolve new moral and ethical equations consistent with humanity's advanced knowledge of what formerly were the mysteries of life. Thanks to genetic science, there are few mysteries any more. They have been disappearing one by one, particularly since James D. Watson and Francis Crick unlocked the secret to living organisms with their discovery of the DNA "double helix," the basic building block of life itself. Thus the great urgency for Catholics, Catholic scientists and moral theologians especially, to be *a part* not *apart* from the science that is shredding life's secrets. Only by being part of the genetics scene can the believing community expect that the astonishing breakthroughs will be fit into solid moral and ethical contexts . . .

CLOSER TO GOD

Today, genetics is still an infant science. Genetic science doubles in knowledge every two years—quantum leaps. We are but at the beginnings of the application of the new knowledge to humanity. As we advance further, some genetic developments are going to defy the imagination; some are likely to unlock secrets we thought reserved to God. In a sense, therefore, we stand on the threshold of a new creation. But we should not be afraid. It is an exciting time to be on earth and to be here as a believer. We should not feel threatened because cells can be fused, because new life can be brought forth in a test tube. Remember, God told us to master the earth and placed no restrictions on the knowledge we were to seek and come by. Indeed, we have a moral obligation to learn as much about life as we can, if only so we can revere it more. We must do this even at the risk that we ourselves will seem to play God. On the other hand, hasn't humankind always played God? The big difference at the moment is that we are getting closer to the Source. Maybe the closer we get, the more wondrous will prove the fact of God.

John Deedy. Photograph by Janet Chinosi Deedy.

In any case, we have no choice but to live in the brave new world of genetics. To turn our backs on this world, to pretend it doesn't exist, is not going to make its challenges go away. We have to be part of it—first, in order to help shape it, second, because humankind for all time stands to benefit from it.

"There's no such thing as 'responsible' engineering of new forms and combinations of life."

Genetic Engineering is "Playing God"

Jeremy Rifkin

Jeremy Rifkin is co-director of the Peoples Business Commission (PBC), an advocacy group which defines key issues facing the world of the future. Genetic engineering is one such issue which Mr. Rifkin and his group believe poses a definite threat to the future of humanity. In the following viewpoint, he focuses upon a Supreme Court decision of June, 1980 granting General Electric the right to create and patent a new type bacteria. He then explains what he sees as the grave dangers involved in that decision.

Consider the following questions while reading:
1. **What human-made life form did the Supreme Court grant General Electric permission to patent?**
2. **According to the author, what will DNA technology eventually accomplish that is contrary to nature?**
3. **According to the author, what has been the position of church leaders regarding genetic engineering?**
4. **Do you agree that genetic engineering could pose a grave threat? Why or why not?**

Jeremy Rifkin, "Playing God", *Sojourners,* August 10, 1980. Reprinted with permission of Sojourners, 1309 L Street NW, Washington, D.C. 20005.

On June 16, 1980, the U.S. Supreme Court ruled, five to four, that human-made life forms may be patented. The decision gave companies the go-ahead to create new forms of life and the right to own and control that life for 17 years under patent law. The case before the court involved a new micro-organism created by a scientist working for General Electric. This particular life form had never before existed in nature. The function of the bug was to eat up oil spills; it had a voracious appetite for oil.

Many things can go wrong with an organism like this. Scientists have no way of knowing how the bug will interact with other life forms in the ecosphere. They can only test it in a laboratory, which can't repeat all the conditions of nature. It might very well be that this bug, once it slurps up the oil, will not die as it is supposed to, but instead grow exponentially and destroy hydrocarbons well beyond oil. It could devastate an entire ecological niche. The possibilities of this happening in any particular case are remote. But the court decision opened the floodgates to thousands and thousands of laboratory-created life forms. One would be hard pressed to guarantee that all of them will be safe . . .

THE DANGERS INVOLVED

Even if genetic engineering were placed firmly under government control, I would still be totally opposed to all aspects of the technology. There are certain technologies in which the inherent dangers are too great regardless of who's controlling it and for what benefit. For example, to believe that nuclear power plants in socialist East Germany are somehow different from nuclear power plants in capitalist West Germany is naive and ridiculous.

I think what we have to learn is that just because a new technology can be done, doesn't necessarily mean it should be done. For too long we've assumed that you can't stop "progress." Well, let's redefine progress.

Let me put the issue in perspective. There have been two major turning points in history in relation to how we organize and manipulate the earth around us. The first was 10,000 years ago when we harnessed fire. For the last 10,000 years we have been recombining all of the non-living matter of the planet into the artifacts of civilization. We call it the age of metals.

In the 1970's, scientists in laboratories were able to take

living material, from unrelated species, and fuse them together, creating new combinations and forms of life that have never before existed in the living gene pool. This is recombinant DNA technology.

A lot of people say, "Isn't this just an extension of things like hybridization and natural breeding and the things we've been doing to intervene in the gene pool for thousands of years?" Absolutely not. With genetic engineering, and specifically with recombinant DNA technology, we can for the

THE CHURCH AND GENETICS

If the church does not have the wherewithal to come out in opposition to the genetic age, then it seems to me that it's time to admit, once and for all, that Christianity has become little more than a permanent apologist for the secular order.

Jeremy Rifkin

first time cross species' boundaries. In nature, a mouse cannot mate with a human being. A carrot cannot mate with an oak tree. Under nature, there are well-established laws that govern separation between families and species. In the few exceptions to this, the offspring is neuter or asexual, like the jackass. But this new technology makes it possible to recombine all the forms of life one wants and make them sexually reproductive. In the book *Who Should Play God?* we quoted many of the major scientists in the field. Most of them said their ultimate aim is human genetic engineering, making the "perfect human being."

While the General Electric bug covered by the court case is not a product of this kind of gene splicing, the industry argued, and the court accepted, the notion that any living thing created by human beings that does not exist in nature and serves some useful function is patentable. The decision laid the legal groundwork for the entire field of recombinant DNA technology.

BIOLOGICAL POLLUTION

There are no nonpolluting technologies. With recombinant DNA, there will be a pollution of a new kind, biological pollution, pollution that grows as the organisms reproduce themselves. You could say that it's a renewable resource, but the pollution from it is renewable, too.

Jonathan King, quoted in *Next,* March/April, 1980

NO REAL BARGAIN

Every single one of these genetic engineering technologies will be looked at as a benefit or a quick fix for someone, somewhere, somehow, under some circumstance. That's the Faustian bargain. The problem is that the totality of these technologies provides a one-way road directly into the brave new world, where we reduce life to its physical components, mechanize it, and bring it under human control and design . . .

This genetic engineering stuff is no longer science fiction. It is quite real. When *Who Should Play God?* was written three years ago, we projected that the first test tube baby would be with us within a handful of years. The scientific community said, "Oh, that's a hundred years away." It happened just two years after we wrote the book. We have to remember that the information in genetics is doubling every 24 months. No science has ever developed this fast.

Having said all this, I do not take it for granted that this technology and the genetic age is a fait accompli. I believe it can be stopped and should be resisted across the board, even knowing that there are certain benefits to be derived. The point is, there's no such thing as "responsible" engineering of new forms and combinations of life . . .

"OF COURSE WE'RE ONLY DOING IT FOR BENEFICIAL PURPOSES."

National Catholic Reporter/Roland Swanson, Jr.

THE CHURCH COMMUNITY

I think the church community is becoming aware of what is at stake with genetic engineering. But it still wants to treat it as a technology that must be looked at with caution . . .

The position of some church leaders has been disappointing up to now. While they have acknowledged that genetic engineering poses grave problems of a theological and moral nature, they are quick to extol what the scientific-corporate establishment has told them will be great possibilities and opportunities forthcoming from this technology. I think that's naive. They haven't learned anything from 30 years of involvement with the so-called peaceful atom.

If the church does not have the wherewithal to come out in opposition to the genetic age, then it seems to me that it's time to admit, once and for all, that Christianity has become little more than a permanent apologist for the secular order.

I have a feeling that many religious leaders think they cannot make a moral or theological decision on this. They say you can't stop science. This is not stopping science, it's stopping genetic engineering. If they can't make a decision to say no to patenting life and engineering the gene pool, then I think there is very little hope for the present Christian leadership.

It could be that the Christian community is just now waking up to this monumental issue, moving it beyond the church's so-called professional ethicists and science experts to the pulpits and parishes. If this is so, we could see a tremendous public reaction against the redesign of God's creation in the corporate laboratories.

"The plain fact is that modern society simply can not survive without its science and technology."

Criticism of Science Hinders Progress

Gerald D. Laubach

Gerald D. Laubach is President and Director of Pfizer, Incorporated, one of the largest pharmaceutical firms in the world. A Ph.D. in chemistry (Massachusetts Institute of Technology, 1950), he frequently contributes scientific articles to technical journals. In the following viewpoint, Dr. Laubach explains why criticism hampers scientific progress and illustrates why he believes such criticism is potentially suicidal to humankind.

Consider the following questions while reading:
1. According to the author, what is the public's current attitude toward science?
2. What arguments does the author offer in favor of modern science?
3. Do you support the author's views? Why or why not?

Gerald D. Laubach, "Growing Criticism of Science Impedes Progress". Reprinted from *USA Today*, July, 1980, pp. 51–53. Copyright 1980 by Society for the Advancement of Education.

From the 16th century to the 1960's, Western man viewed science as progress itself. Expressing this view, Philip Handler, president of the National Academy of Sciences, said: "Scientific inquiry has challenged the dogma of an authoritarian world for the last 400 years . . ."

Today, science is being challenged in turn by those who seemingly seek comfort in authoritarian restraints on the search for knowledge . . .

PUBLIC DISTRUST

A nationally-syndicated cartoon I saw last Easter summed up this anti-science tendency of the times in a few quick strokes. The cartoon was of mankind crucified on a cross of technology. This was followed a few weeks later by a headline in a major daily newspaper, which read: "Nuclear Accident Aggravates the Public's Distrust of Assurances from Experts on Technical Topics." The message, however misguided, was clear—science and scientists are not to be trusted.

I don't want to overstate my case. Both cartoons and newswriting may be art forms in which hyperbole is expected, or even encouraged. Nor are science and technology without their blemishes, without their mistakes and human frailties. Still, William F. Buckley reminds us that, while not perfect, "The record of the scientists, whether in medicine or in construction, or in energy research, is infinitely better than that of the non-scientists in their own professions."

There are countless instances throughout history where science, even with its imperfections, was right and human instincts were wrong. Passionate fears were aroused with the advent of steam power and electricity, surgery and immunology, and the automobile and air travel. Those who fear the unknown have been all too willing to repeat the Inquisition's sins against Galileo. Fortunately, since the Age of Enlightenment, reason has, for the most part, prevailed.

These caveats aside, I believe the steady stream of alarmist, anti-science news of recent years nourishes, as much as it reflects, a growing anti-science cast in society as a whole— one that bodes ill for both science and society . . .

ACCOMPLISHMENTS OF SCIENCE

The anti-science, anti-progress mood spreads as objective reasoning shrinks. The allegations against science have tended to ignore its extraordinary accomplishments and its potential. The plain fact is that modern society simply can not survive without its science and technology. Indeed, without them, Western economies can not prosper and can not provide a better life to both their own people and to the people of the Third World. Earth resources satellites, for example, have provided, vastly improved data for development planning in agriculture and forestry around the world. Modern medicines are being used to fight widespread diseases. Hunger and disease, which know no national boundaries, are being challenged by the improving products of science. The politicians, the convincers, the office-holders— not scientists—determine the extent to which the products of science are used and how . . .

Even our universities—bastions of academic freedom— have not been immune to the imposition of politically motivated controls on their research activities. A striking case in point was the very nearly successful campaign a year or two ago to write a Federal law that would have brought academic molecular biologists under truly Draconian controls. Here was a case where the concerns of a few scientists about so-called recombinant DNA research, a kind of genetic engineering, were systematically exaggerated by a vocal minority seemingly bent on denying society the potential benefits of a fundamental new discovery. It is research that promises entirely new approaches in the fight against disease and to meet the world's food and energy needs. Yet, we were nearly denied that promise . . .

THE GLORY OF ACHIEVEMENT

It is good for man to do his best, to come nearer godhead through the knowledge of what it means to be vulnerable and capable of achievement; he searches after beauty, erecting dream castles upon the arid plain.

Brad Linaweaver, *New Guard*, March, 1976

PROGRESS OR SUICIDE?

In Western societies, the power and productivity of science has sprung largely from its pluralism and its consequent freedom. History reminds us that constant vigilance is required if we are to avoid the perilous consequences of attempts by society or a misguided few to determine what is permissible to know and what is illicit to learn. Attempts to restrain the search for knowledge have often proved to be more frightening than the scenarios constructed by the prophets of doom and gloom themselves. To cut off research because of fear of the possibilities inherent in knowledge is to condemn our society to a life without creativity, without new capabilities. It would be a suicidal policy.

"The great insight into the mechanisms of life...can make us see humans and life itself as so much machinery."

Criticism of Science is Sometimes Necessary

Paul Schimmel

Paul Schimmel has authored numerous articles on scientific subjects. A professor of biochemistry and biophysics at the Massachusetts Institute of Technology, he believes that the technology of genetic engineering should not be separated from Christian ethics. In the following viewpoint, Professor Schimmel explains why basic Christian beliefs must remain a corollary of the new technology.

Consider the following questions while reading:

1. According to the author, why must we be concerned about "the power to manipulate these (genetic) mechanisms in extraordinary ways?"
2. Do you believe that the author shows unnecessary concern? Why or why not?

Paul Schimmel, "Genetic Engineering: Blessing or Curse?", *Christianity Today,* June 2, 1978. Copyright ©by Christianity Today, 1978 and used by permission.

Genetic engineering has sparked more controversy than any scientific subject since the birth of the nuclear age in the 1940s. Scientists, congressmen, and citizens' groups have hotly debated man's newfound power to manipulate genetic material. These genes form something like a set of blueprints. It determines all of the hereditary characteristics of an organism.

Nothing is more fundamental to life than genes and heredity. We know that differences between various life forms, such as birds, insects, and plants are due to genetic differences. And we all know how many of our own characteristics are fixed by what we inherited from our parents. Thus, when scientists toy with genetic material, it's the same as manipulating life itself. It's perhaps the greatest act in the game of man attempting to "play God." And the implications of genetic engineering for Christians and non-Christians alike are profound . . .

IMPORTANT QUESTIONS

Christians cannot avoid some pointed theological issues raised by the current fascination with self-guided evolution...What does it mean to be created in God's image if we select and shape human intelligence and personality? Will our belief in a spiritual and transcendent reality be shattered with the advent of human engineering?

Editorial, *Christianity Today,* January 19, 1979

BOTH BENEFITS AND DANGERS

We must think about the implications of this new technology. For years to come there will be a concern about whether, in the course of time and of large scale genetic experimentation, living organisms will be adversely affected by an unfavorable restructuring of the balance of nature. There is little to say about this possibility; we don't know enough. But it behooves us to be sensitive to the possibilities and to act with discrete and conscientious concern should we become aware of a worrisome situation.

There is no question that genetic engineering has spiritual ramifications. It's one of a long series of scientific advances that shifts thinking from the metaphysical to the physical. It takes some of the mystery out of life. This is not to say that this is bad or that we shouldn't try to understand life and nature with penetrating scientific insight. But if we substitute that insight for faith in and mystical reverence for the God behind it all, then we've lost something.

What's more, we have to worry that the great insight into the mechanisms of life and the power to manipulate these mechanisms in extraordinary ways can make us see humans and life itself as so much machinery. It can boil down to a distraction from the concept of a human as a child of God, with special spiritual endowments. This is not the fault of genetic engineering or of any other technology; it's simple human short-sightedness. And here Christians can bring a sensitive spiritual perspective to the issues at hand.

Genetic engineering is an extraordinary achievement of science and technology. The potential benefits are immense, but there are enough dangers and unknowns that it could become a curse instead of a blessing. Which it will be depends upon the conscientious participation of all of us in the decisions that govern this activity. Christians must maintain a spiritual perspective and encourage that perspective among others. In these ways, we can assure that our scientific explorations into genetics bring the blessings they're intended to give.

"The birth of Louise Brown...amounts to a nice object lesson in the compatibility of advanced 'human engineering' and traditional human values like procreation."

Test-Tube Babies Are a Blessing

Pittsburgh Post-Gazette

The successful birth of Louise Brown sparked a world-wide media circus. In newspapers and on radio and TV, debates regarding the scientific and ethical implications of the world's first "test-tube baby" were paraded before the international public. The furor continues and more than likely will continue with the same passion with which issues like abortion were met. On July 28, 1978, the Pittsburgh Post-Gazette ran an editorial which concluded by noting that "the Brown's blessed event suggests that an exaggerated fear of such research and innovation can itself do harm to human values." The following viewpoint is the unedited version of that editorial.

Consider the following questions while reading:

1. **Why was Mrs. Brown unable to conceive and what procedures did her doctors follow to remedy her problem?**
2. **According to the *New England Journal of Medicine*, what additional medical benefits may come as a result of the successful birth of Britain's Louise Brown?**

Editorial page, *Pittsburgh Post-Gazette*, July 28, 1978. Reprinted by permission.

The birth of 5-pound, 12-ounce Louise Brown, Britain's photogenic "test-tube baby," could not have come at a more fortuitous time for the cause of controversial scientific research. Only a few months ago, such research had to weather a public-relations disaster when an American author claimed that a child had been cloned from the cells of an egocentric millionaire. The cloning report, which medical experts denounced as a hoax, reinforced the popular notion — derived mostly from Grade-B science-fiction films — that reproduction-related research inevitably leads to bizarre and inhuman results.

A NORMAL CHILD

There was nothing bizarre about the plight of Mr. and Mrs. Gilbert John Brown of Oldham, England, the world's first "test-tube parents." A conventional working-class couple, they wanted to have children, but were unable to because of a defect in Mrs. Brown's fallopian tubes. The Browns were offered hope by two experts in embryology who had been painstakingly researching the feasibility of "test-tube" conceptions for years. The doctors removed a ripe egg from Mrs. Brown's ovary, placed it in a laboratory dish, and then fertilized it with sperm taken from her husband. The egg was re-implanted in Mrs. Brown's uterus and continued to grow and differentiate like any other human embryo. The birth this week of an apparently normal child was the dramatic culmination of a daring new procedure. But in human terms, the medical "miracle" was reassuringly familiar. A husband and wife were aided by methodical and cautious scientists to achieve a perfectly natural goal: parenthood. In principle, the "test-tube" birth was no more "unnatural" than thousands of births produced by artificial insemination.

The widely publicized birth of Louise Brown — and the fact that her parents were such benign sorcerers' apprentices — amount to a nice object lesson in the compatibility of advanced "human engineering" and traditional human values like procreation. Another impeccably traditional value, the prevention and cure of pain and disease, animates another sort of scientific research which is often criticized in apocalyptic terms — genetic medicine. This week that sub-specialty produced its own front-page news. The New England Journal of Medicine reported that, for the first time, doctors have been able to identify a single gene among the millions in a microscopic human cell. As with any laboratory breakthrough — including "test-tube" conception, which required a decade of study and experimentation before it succeeded — the isolation of the gene may not produce therapeutic results for years. But the discovery may enable doctors to identify the presence of genetic disorders in fetuses and even—after more research—correct such defects surgically.

There is undoubtedly an element of serendipity in the favorable reaction to the "test-tube baby." Had the child been born with a birth defect—even one unrelated to the mode of her conception—the public response would have been quite different. But, largely owing to the care and patience of the doctors involved, the procedure was a success. And allowing for some predictable fretting about whether the "test-tube" birth opens the way to a *Brave New World*-style society, public opinion has seemed to recognize that the doctors who helped the Browns to become parents were no mad scientists.

A FREE CHOICE

To say that a person is wrong to bring a child into the world differently than you would do it is arrogant.

Brad Linaweaver, *New Guard,* March, 1976

EXAGGERATED FEAR

Medical experimentation is not without its social risks and ethical dilemmas. For that reason, professional medical-ethics bodies are right to monitor such research carefully. But the Gilbert Browns' well-publicized blessed event suggests that an exaggerated fear of such research and innovation can itself do harm to human values.

"Blinded mankind has been trying to find the way to true happiness by experimenting – with very little success."

Test–Tube Babies Violate God's Laws

Clayton Steep

A native of Milwaukee, Wisconsin, Clayton Steep attended the University of Wisconsin for two years, then transferred to Ambassador College, Pasadena, California, where he majored in theology. For the past 25 years, he has been involved in the religious publications field. He is currently on the staff of *The Plain Truth* magazine. In the following viewpoint, Mr. Steep outlines his ethical, legal and moral objections to test–tube babies.

Consider the following questions while reading:
1. **List and explain some of the problems the author fears may result from manipulating human reproduction.**
2. **How do the author's views differ from those in the previous viewpoint? Who do you believe has a stronger argument? Explain your answer.**

Bouncy little Louise Brown—soon to be 2 years old—is an apparently normal and healthy child, though her life began in a 1-by-2-inch glass tube.

For Mr. and Mrs. John Brown of Bristol, England, the birth of Louise was the realization of a dream. After all, three years previously they had been told by doctors that they could never have a child. Then they were referred to Doctors Patrick Steptoe and Robert Edwards, who successfully brought about Louise's conception in a glass tube . . .

Dr. Steptoe plans soon to engineer the birth of a human child to a surrogate mother. In other words, a human embryo, which has been conceived in a laboratory, is to be put into the womb of a female "third person"—not the woman who supplied the egg. If the experiment is successful, the child will be born to a woman who is not its real mother . . .

DISTURBING QUESTIONS

Volumes have been written debating the pros and cons of the rapidly expanding field of biomedicine. Some warn of a monstrous moral, ethical and legal genie that cannot be forced back into the test tube. They denounce the spector of technicians with culture dishes creating new life forms or making God-like decisions concerning the life, death and likeness of human beings.

Concerning the work already being done with human cells, there are indeed profoundly disturbing questions. For example, what happens if a 7-day-old embryo in a glass tube is found to be defective? Does it still have a "right to life"? When is a human embryo human? What if defects don't show up until the baby is born? Vance Packard, in his book, *The People Shapers*, asks: "If we permit the implant of *in vitro* human embryos in women, are we prepared to kill monsters, imbeciles and hopelessly defective humans born from such research?"

"I think the potential is there for serious anomalies should an unqualified scientist mishandle an embryo," Dr. John Marlow, an American gynecologist who observed the Steptoe-Edwards experiment first hand, remarked in *U.S. News and World Report* (Aug. 7, 1978). Many ask just who is going to police all the "unqualified" scientists in the world.

The legal ramifications of manipulated human reproduction will be immense. How can a person conceived artificially ever find his true "roots"? Who is he really? Exactly *who is* a baby born from a surrogate mother? Who is legally responsible for the child? . . .

Again from Dr. Marlow: "I think what has been done in Britain [test-tube fertilization] poses many problems to society, and some of our traditional and very important concepts of mother, father, child will be challenged *(ibid.)*.

"We're on a slippery slope," cautioned geneticist Robert J. Berry. "Western society is built around the family; once you divorce sex from procreation, what happens to the family?" (*Time,* July 31, 1978).

Regarding the effect surrogate mothers would have on the family institution, *U.S. News and World Report* (Aug. 7, 1978) stated: "Beyond the legal entaglements are fundamental questions about how this will affect the mother–child relationship and the early bonding that social anthropologists have considered so important to child development.

"At the same time, surrogate pregnancy is seen as a final step in the biological liberation of woman. This could have a widening impact on the role of women in terms of jobs and education as the sexual gap between men and women narrows. Like men, women could 'sire' children without the responsibility of pregnancy and childbirth . . ."

PROBLEMS ARE RAISED

What has been done in Britain poses many problems to society, and some of our traditional and very important concepts of mother, father, child will be challenged.

John L. Marlow, M.D., quoted in *U.S. News and World Report*

IS RESTRAINT POSSIBLE?

Dr. Leon Kass, biochemist and professor at the University of Chicago, has expressed misgivings that so many steps have already been taken—with the best of intentions. "At least one good humanitarian reason can be found to justify each step," he says. "The first step serves as a precedent for the second and the second for the third, not just technolo-

MOTHER AND CHILD

gically but also in moral arguments. Perhaps a wise society would say to infertile couples: 'We understand your sorrow, but it might be better not to go ahead and do this'" (*Newsweek*, Aug. 7, 1978).

But he has noted, "It is hard to speak about restraint in a culture that seems to venerate very little above man's attempt to master all."

Man's attempt to master all. That is what we are really dealing with. Notice this: "To restrict cloning–related research would mean closing the door on an important area of knowledge. To continue to probe the secrets of the cell, however, is perhaps to uncover the secret of human cloning. And, given the nature of man, if it can be done, it will be done" ("Clones: Will There Be 'Carbon Copy' People?" *The Reader's Digest*, March, 1979). Compare that last sentence with Genesis 11:6: "Now nothing will be restrained from them [mankind]."

"The issue is how far we play God," complained British MP Leo Abse at the time of Louise Brown's birth.

THE WORLD'S FIRST "HUMAN EXPERIMENTATION"

The Bible records the very first experimentation by humans. God had provided in the Garden of Eden for the first humans' every need—physical, material and spiritual. It was not necessary for them to experiment for themselves in order to find the best way to live. All they had to do was obey His laws and they could have lived abundant lives, free from want, unhappiness and suffering. The "tree of life" symbolized God's way—the way that leads to eternal life . . .

The disobedience of Adam and Eve cut them and all their descendants off from God. Ever since that time, blinded mankind has been trying to find the way to true happiness by experimenting—with very little success.

Not only has mankind not found happiness after nearly 6,000 years of experimentation, but as a result of man's experiments, he is about to reap the whirlwind in the form of a cataclysmic time of tribulation that will come close to annihilating all life from planet Earth (Matthew 24:21–22).

DISTINGUISHING BETWEEN FACT AND OPINION

This discussion activity is designed to promote experimentation with one's ability to distinguish between fact and opinion. Consider the following example. Virtually everyone will agree that the earth is the fifth largest planet of our solar system and that it is the only planet *definitely* known to support animal life. Relying upon recent findings, this is a verifiable fact. However, when we deal with the question of beginnings, we enter the realm of opinion. To date, no one, scientist or theologian, has been able to demonstrate the ultimate origins of the earth and the life forms it supports. Therefore, in the absence of verifiable evidence, the problems of planetary and life origins remain an opinion.

PART I

Instructions

Some of the following statements are taken from this book and some have other origins. Consider each statement carefully. Mark *O* for any statement you feel is an opinion or interpretation of facts. Mark *F* for any statement you believe is a fact. Then discuss and compare your judgments with those of other class members.

O = Opinion
F = Fact

_____ 1. The supernatural has no support in science.

_____ 2. Prehistorical humans invented gods to answer the mysteries of nature, and invented religions as a means to influence divine will.

_____ 3. We live in an expanding universe, in which all the galaxies around us are moving apart from us and one another at enormous speeds.

_____ 4. Both evolution and creation are theories.

_____ 5. It takes more faith to believe in evolution than creation.

_____ 6. Special creationism is irrational in principle and, therefore, not admissible as a scientific doctrine.

_____ 7. There is no intrinsic conflict between faith and science, between God the creator and evolutionary theory.

_____ 8. Genetic research is indeed moral. In fact, the immorality would be neglect or prohibition of this research.

_____ 9. Modern society cannot survive without its science and technology.

_____ 10. Many scientists have been and can be devout believers in a Divine Creator.

_____ 11. If the universe was not created by chance, it must have been created by God.

_____ 12. Once it is proven that evolution is fact and not theory, people will no longer be able to believe in God.

PART II

Instructions

STEP 1

The class should break into groups of four to six students.

STEP 2

Each small group should try to locate two statements of fact and two statements of opinion in this book.

STEP 3

Each group should choose a student to record its statements.

STEP 4

The class should discuss and compare the small groups' statements.

BIBLIOGRAPHY

The editors have compiled the following list of periodical articles which deal with the subject matter of this chapter. The majority of periodicals listed are available in most school and public libraries.

Frederick Ausubel, Jon Beckwith and Kaaren Janssen — *The Politics of Genetic Engineering: Who Decides Who's Defective?*, **Psychology Today,** June, 1974, p. 30.

The Christian Century — *The Government's New Bioethics Commission,* June 4–11, 1980, p. 630.

Christianity Today — *Human Engineering: Trouble Ahead,* January 19, 1979, p. 12.

Lee Colman and Trudy Solomon — *Big Brother Knows Best,* **Psychology Today,** November, 1976, p. 85.

Commonweal — *Test-Tube Ethics,* March 2, 1979, p. 101.

Craig W. Ellison — *Engineering Humans,* **Christianity Today,** January 19, 1979, p. 15.

George H. Fried — *Cloning - The Promise and the Threat,* **USA Today,** September, 1979, p. 58.

P. Gwynne — *Caution: Gene Transplants,* **Newsweek,** March 21, 1977, p. 57.

S. Loebl — *Beyond the Test-Tube Babies: Is Embryo Transfer Next?,* **Science Digest,** November, 1979, p. 24.

Henry McDonald — *Implanting Human Values into Genetic Control,* **Science and Public Affairs,** February, 1974, p. 21.

Arno G. Motulsky — *Doomsaying Genetically: The Fear Is Groundless,* **Science Digest,** August, 1979, p. 20.

M. Reisner — *DNA: Will the Future Curse Science's Decisions Today?* **Science Digest,** July, 1977, p. 62.

Jeremy Rifkin — *One Small Step beyond Mankind,* **The Progressive,** March, 1977, p. 21.

C. Rubenstein — *Little-Known Hazards of AID: Disease, Inbreeding, Guilt,* **Psychology Today,** May, 1980, p. 23.

Science News — *Test-Tube Babies and the Law,* June 2, 1979, p. 358.

Time — *Shaping Life in the Lab,* March 9, 1981, p. 50.

John V. Tunney and Meldon E. Levine — *Genetic Engineering,* **Saturday Review,** August 5, 1972, p. 23.

Index

emotion, 23-24
energy, 46, 48, 61, 97, 122
environment, 23, 73, 81, 111
eternal, 46, 134
ethical, 33, 112, 127, 129, 130-131,
  ethics, 22-24, 119, 124, 129
euglena, 26
evidence, 21, 45-46, 48-49, 61, 63,
  71, 74-76, 78, 82, 84, 86-88, 89-90,
  97-99
evolution, 15-17, 61, 70-73, 74-76,
  78, 79-80, 83, 84-89, 90, 92, 94,
  96-99, 100-104, 125
existence, 26-27, 32, 35, 37, 49, 60,
  72, 75, 89, 97-98, 117
experience, 21, 23-24, 26, 35, 37,
  56, 79, 82, 86, 89, 94, 112
experiment, 15-16, 21, 24, 26, 37,
  72-73, 85-86, 89, 112, 125, 128-129,
  130-131, 134
exploitation, 27
extinct, 87, 90

faith, 16-17, 22-23, 26-27, 32, 35, 37,
  48, 50, 52, 71, 74, 76, 80, 89, 92,
  95, 100-101, 126
Faustian, 117
federal government, 23
fetus, 22, 129
force, 16, 35-36, 45, 48, 78, 102, 112
free (freedom), 24, 79, 83, 92, 101,
  122-123, 129, 134
fundamentalist, 72, 80-82, 94, 101

Galilei, Galileo, 15, 24, 92, 95, 104,
  121
Genesis, 16, 45-46, 53, 55, 81-82, 92,
  94-95, 100-102, 104, Genesis 11:6,
  134
genetic, 81-82, 110-113, 114-119,
  122, 124-126, 128-129, 132
God, 17, 21, 23, 25-27, 32, 34, 37,
  38, 44-45, 49, 51-53, 55, 60-63, 78,
  81-82, 92, 94, 97-98, 100-104,
  110-113, 114, 117, 119, 122,
  124-126, 130-131, 134
gods, 102

heaven, 15, 27, 45-46, 49, 53, 95,
  101
hell, 27
hereditary, 125
heresy, 15
hoax, 128
hominids, 99
Hoyle, Fred, 61
human, 16, 22-24, 27, 30, 32-33, 49,
  55, 61, 63, 75-76, 78, 88, 94,
  98-99, 102, 104, 110-113, 114-115,

117, 121, 124-126, 127-129,
  130-131, 134
humanist, 79, 82, 97
Huxley, Thomas, 35
hypothesis (hypothetical), 24, 26,
  71

immaculate conception, 22
immoral, 24, 110-112
infinite (infinity), 59, 61-62
information, 21-22
inquiry, 22, 24, 50, 61, 83, 121
Inquisition, 15, 121
irrational, 61, 79, 82

Jastrow, Robert, 51-52, 55, 57,
  picture, 47, viewpoint, 44-50
Jehovah, 23
Jesus Christ, 24, 27
Jewish (Jews), 22, 92, 102, 111

Koran, 22

legal, 24, 117, 130-132
logic, 23, 74-75, 82
Lyell, Sir Charles (geologist), 80

Malthus, Thomas R. (economist),
  80
matter, 35, 37, 45-46, 48, 57, 61, 75,
  86, 92, 96, 98, 115
metaphysical, 27, 126
miracles, 22, 26-27, 128
Mohammedanism, 24
moral, 30, 33, 110-113, 118-119,
  130-131, 134
Mormon, 23, Mormonism, 23-24
mutation, 73, 76, 81, 87, 89-90, 97
mystery (mysterious), 16, 29, 32,
  34-35, 37-38, 46, 49, 50, 61, 112,
  126, mystical, 94, 126
myths, 22

nature, 16, 20-22, 28, 30, 32, 35, 38,
  49, 55, 61, 79, 81, 87, 102-104,
  114-115, 117-118, 125-126, 134
natural, 33, 48, 80-82, 95, 111, 116,
  128, natural forces, 23, natural
  selection, 73, 80-81

observation, 15-16, 21, 35, 37, 57,
  85-86, 89
O'Hair, Madalyn Murray, 29, 32
opinion, 26, 30, 34, 57, 129
oracles, 23
organisms, 26, 71-73, 80, 86, 88-90,
  112, 114, 117, 125
origins, 16, 21, 35, 46, 49, 70-73,
  74, 79, 81, 83, 85, 88-90, 97-99,

140

MEET THE EDITORS

David L. Bender is a history graduate from the University of Minnesota. He also has a M.A. in government from St. Mary's University in San Antonio, Texas. He has taught social problems at the high school level for several years. He is the general editor of the Opposing Viewpoints Series and has authored most of the titles in the series.

Bruno Leone received his B.A. (Phi Kappa Phi) from Arizona State University and his M.A. in history from the University of Minnesota. A Woodrow Wilson Fellow (1967), he is currently an instructor at Minneapolis Community College, Minneapolis, Minnesota, where he has taught history, anthropology, and political science. In 1974-75, he was awarded a Fellowship by the National Endowment for the Humanities to research the intellectual origins of American Democracy.